*TO JILL*

# NATURE

## AN ILLUSTRATED GUIDE TO
## COMMON PLANTS AND ANIMALS

# ALBERTA

## JAMES KAVANAGH

### ILLUSTRATIONS BY MARIANNE NAKASKA
### LINDA DUNN AND HORST H. KRAUSE

LONE
PINE

**The Publishers:**
*Lone Pine Publishing*
206, 10426-81st Avenue
Edmonton, Alberta, Canada
T6E 1X5

## Canadian Cataloguing in Publication Data
Kavanagh, James, 1960-
    Nature Alberta
Includes bibliographical reference and index.
ISBN 0-919433-91-X

1. Zoology-- Alberta.  2. Animals--Identification.
3. Botany--Alberta.  4. Plants--Identification.
I. Nakaska, Marianne.  II. Krause, Horst, 1951-
III. Dunn, Linda.  IV. Title.
QH106.2.A4K39 1991    574.97123   C91-091135-5


Cover and layout design: *Beata Kurpinski*
Illustration: *Marianne Nakaska, Linda Dunn, Horst H.Krause*
Mapping: *Rick Checkland*
Editorial: *Elaine Butler, Jane Spalding, Phillip Kennedy*
Printing: *Kyodo Printing Co. (S'pore) Pte. Ltd., Singapore*


The publisher gratefully acknowledges the assistance of the Federal Department of Communications, Alberta Culture and Multiculturalism, the Canada Council, and the Alberta Foundation for the Literary Arts in the publication of this book.

# CONTENTS

# PREFACE

This book has been written in response to the need for a layman's guide to common species of plants and animals in Alberta. Though there are already several field guides on the market which serve as identification guides to our local flora and fauna, many of these are too complicated and too detailed to be of use to the novice in the field.

Because this guide has been written for the lay person, every effort has been made to simplify the presentation of the material. Descriptions, illustrations, and distribution maps are grouped together for ease of reference, and technical terms have been held to a minimum throughout. A complete index of common and scientific names is included in the back as a further aid to finding information quickly.

The content should in no way be interpreted as a comprehensive overview of Alberta's flora and fauna. It is merely intended to provide basic information on some common species, in order to interest as wide an audience as possible in the fascinating and distinctive nature of our province.

I would like to acknowledge and express my grateful thanks to all who contributed to this guide. For their help in selecting species and guiding the initial layout and design of the book, thanks to Hugh Smith, Julie Hrapko, and Bruce McGillivray of the Provincial Museum of Alberta, Anne Smreciu and Jim Dau of Alberta Environment Services, Joe Nelson, Randy Bayer, Jan Murie, and Dave Boag of the University of Alberta, Ellen Gasser and Monica Keith of the Calgary Zoo, Harold Pinel of the Ingelwood Bird Sanctuary and Tony Daffern and Grant Kennedy. Special thanks to Elaine Butler, Ellen Gasser, Anne Smreciu, Harold Pinel, Mary Walters Riskin and Jill Kavanagh for their assistance in editing the manuscript, and for their practical and technical assistance in my day-to-day efforts. Thanks to Dr. David Suzuki for allowing me to reprint his essay. For help with maps, I'm indebted to Ronald Whistance-Smith of the University of Alberta, Bruce Waddell and Denis Hoybak of Maps Alberta, and J.J. Nowicki of Alberta Recreation and Parks. Others who helped in reading the text, checking art, and suggesting improvements include Jane Wilson, Keith Dundas, John Belisle and Kristen. Lastly I would like to thank my family for their undying enthusiasm and support and for believing in this project from the start. Thank you all.

J. D. K.

# INTRODUCTION

*By Dr. David Suzuki*

*An internationally renowned geneticist and environmentalist, Dr. Suzuki has heightened our experience and understanding of nature over the years through numerous books, articles, and television programs.*

In spite of the vast expanse of wilderness in this country, most Canadian children grow up in urban settings. In other words, they live in a world conceived, shaped and dominated by other people. Even the farms located around cities and towns are carefully groomed and landscaped for human convenience. There's nothing wrong with that, of course, but in such an environment, it's very easy to lose any sense of connection with nature.

In city apartments and dwellings, the presence of cockroaches, fleas, ants, mosquitoes or houseflies is guaranteed to elicit the spraying of insecticides. Mice and rats are poisoned or trapped, while the gardeners wage a never-ending struggle with ragweed, dandelions, slugs and root-rot. We have a modern arsenal of chemical weapons to fight off these invaders and we use them lavishly.

We worry when kids roll in the mud or wade through a puddle because they'll get "dirty." Children learn attitudes and values very quickly and the lesson in cities is very clear — nature is an enemy, it's dirty, dangerous or a nuisance. So youngsters learn to distance themselves from nature and try to control it. I am astonished at the number of adults who loathe or are terrified by snakes, spiders, butterflies, worms, birds — the list seems endless.

If you reflect on the history of humankind, you realize that for 99 per cent of our species' existence on the planet, we were deeply embedded in and dependent on nature. When plants and animals were plentiful, we flourished. When famine and drought struck, our numbers fell accordingly. We remain every bit as dependent on nature today — we need plants to fix photons of energy into sugar molecules and to cleanse the air and replenish the oxygen. It is folly to forget our dependence on an intact ecosystem. But we do whenever we teach our offspring to fear or detest the natural world. The urban message kids get runs completely counter to what they are born with, a natural interest in other life forms. Just watch a child in a first encounter with a flower or ant — there is an instant interest and fascination. We condition them out of it.

The result is that when my 7-year-old daughter brings home new friends, they invariably recoil in fear or disgust when she tries to show them her favorite pets — three beautiful salamanders that her grandfather got for her in Vancouver. And when my 3-year-old comes wandering in with her treasures — millipedes, spiders, slugs and sowbugs that she catches under rocks lining the front lawn — children and adults usually respond by saying "yuk."

I can't overemphasize the tragedy of that attitude. For, inherent in this view is the assumption that human beings are special and different and that we lie outside nature. Yet it is this belief that is creating many of our environmental problems today.

Does it matter whether we sense our place in nature so long as we have cities and technology? Yes, and for many reasons, not the least of which is that virtually all scientists were fascinated with nature as children and retained that curiousity throughout their lives. But a far more important reason is that if we retain a spiritual sense of connection with all other life-forms, it can't help but profoundly affect the way we act. Whenever my daughter sees a picture of an animal dead or dying, she asks me fearfully, "Daddy, are there any more?" At 7 years, she already knows about extinction and it frightens her.

The yodel of a loon at sunset, the vast flocks of migrating waterfowl in the fall, the indomitable salmon returning thousands of kilometres — these images of nature have inspired us to create music, poetry and art. And when we struggle to retain a handful of California condors or whooping cranes, it's clearly not from a fear of ecological collapse, it's because there is something obscene and frightening about the disappearance of another species at our hands.

If children grow up understanding that we are animals, they will look at other species with a sense of fellowship and community. If they understand their ecological place — the biosphere — then when children see the great virgin forests of the Queen Charlotte Islands being clearcut, they will feel physical pain, because they will understand that those trees are an extension of themselves.

When children who know their place in the ecosystem see factories spewing poison into the air, water and soil, they will feel ill because someone has violated their home. This is not mystical mumbo-jumbo. We have poisoned the life support systems that sustain all organisms because we have lost a sense of ecological place. Those of us who are parents have to realize the unspoken, negative lessons we are conveying to our children. Otherwise, they will continue to desecrate this planet as we have.

It's not easy to avoid giving these hidden lessons. I have struggled to cover my dismay and queasiness when Severn and Sarika come running in with a large wolf spider or when we've emerged from a ditch covered with leeches or when they have been stung accidentally by yellowjackets feeding on our left-overs. But that's nature. I believe efforts to teach our children to love and respect other life forms are priceless.

(Reprinted with permission of the author. Previously appeared in the *Globe & Mail*, 2/7/87.)

# HOW TO USE THIS BOOK

This book is an identification guide for 330 of the more common species of plants and animals found in Alberta. Included are many familiar and important species, and some which are less familiar but no less interesting. Some common foreign species which are widespread throughout the province have also been included.

In order to make this guide useful in the field, the illustrations, text, and distribution maps for each species are grouped together. In many instances, the illustrations alone may be sufficient for making a positive identification.

**Illustrations** - Many species show colour variations because of sex, age, time of year, and environment. For ease of reference, they have been illustrated in their most prevalent colouration. Illustrations of animals, for example, usually feature the adult male in its breeding colouration.

**Text** - For each species, the text includes reference to its common and scientific names, average total length (animals) or height (plants) of mature organisms, habitat, key field marks, distinguishing behavioural characteristics, and items of general interest.

**Distribution Maps** - These maps indicate the approximate geographic range of species throughout the province. It should be noted that species are not evenly distributed within their range, and the reader should use the habitat description in the text to pinpoint the areas where they are likely to occur.

While the classes are presented in the reverse of taxonomic order, the species in each class are in taxonomic order. Exceptions have been made in some cases to group different species according to superficial characteristics, in order to aid novices in field identification. The American Coot, for example, which belongs in the order of cranes and their allies (*Gruiformes)*, has been grouped with ducks since it is duck-like in looks and habit, and is often found in the presence of ducks. Wildflowers have been arranged by colour, because research has shown this arrangement makes more obvious sense to amateurs than evolutionary ordering. The species checklists in the back of the book have been arranged in scientific order. Exceptions are noted where they occur in the text, and those interested can refer to the checklists to determine proper evolutionary ordering.

The best way to learn and recognize the plants and animals in Alberta is simply by practice. When you are hiking or travelling, get into the habit of carrying a field guide with you and noting the plants or animals along the way. There are no tried and true methods of field identification, since each person's pattern of observation and learning is different. As you gain experience, you'll develop your own techniques for making quick and accurate observations. Don't be afraid to mark up the book and underline the characteristics that are most helpful to you.

The beauty of this fascinating pastime is that the more that you learn, the more pleasure and satisfaction you'll be able to derive from it. As this is only an introductory guide, you'll probably want to supplement it at some point with more comprehensive information on your favourite area of interest. A list of references has been included at the back of the book to aid in further study.

# NATURAL REGIONS

The distribution of plants and animals throughout the province is largely determined by the climate, geography and soil conditions in each area. The conditions in each region dictate the kinds of vegetation it can support, and this, in turn, directly affects the distribution of animals. Alberta is commonly divided into the following natural regions:

## GRASSLAND

The grassland is located in southeastern Alberta in the warmest and driest part of the province. Grasses grow better than trees in this area because of poor soil conditions and high winds. Rainfall is normally low, and the vegetation is primarily composed of drought-resistant species including grasses, cacti and mat-forming shrubs. Much of our native grassland has been converted to farmland for planting cereal crops and grazing livestock. Shrubs and trees occur mostly in ravines and along waterways, though stands of poplars become more common as one moves north and west. Once the domain of the bison, the area supports numerous mammals, birds and the majority of reptiles found in the province.

## PARKLAND

The parkland occurs north of the grasslands and consists of grassland alternating with groves of trees. The soil is rich and supports a wide variety of vegetation. Aspen and balsam poplar are the dominant tree species. Associated with the tree groves are numerous varieties of shrubs including willows, gooseberry, buckbrush, dogwood, silverberry and wild roses. Though the parkland region is located primarily in central Alberta, small islands of parkland also occur in the northern boreal forest in the Peace River region.

## BOREAL FOREST

The boreal forest is our largest natural region, encompassing much of the northern half of the province. From transitional parkland in the south to subarctic woodland in the north, it includes a wide variety of habitats. Covered with mostly coniferous forest, characteristic tree species include White Spruce on uplands, Black Spruce on lowlands, and Jack Pine on light sandy soil. Deciduous species including aspen, Balsam Poplar and White Birch dominate the southern part of the region, but decrease in number as one moves north.

## MONTANE

The montane region is a transitional zone reaching from the forested uplands at the foot of the Rockies to the drier lowlands in the east. The vegetation at upper elevations is dominated by coniferous species including white and black spruce, pines and junipers. These are replaced by deciduous species at lower elevations including aspen, poplar, and paper birch. Alders, willows, Labrador Tea, Bunchberry, Red Paintbrush and Fireweed are common undergrowth species throughout much of the region.

## ROCKY MOUNTAINS

Though seemingly dominated by coniferous forests, the Rockies support a diverse array of plants, depending on the altitude, slope and exposure of a given area. The lower slopes are characterized by the presence of Limber Pine, Lodgepole Pine, Engelmann Spruce and White Spruce. Drier sites support aspen groves and grassland. Nearer to the treeline, Whitebark Pine and Alpine Larch are common, as are a diversity of cold-resistant shrubs and wildflowers.

## CANADIAN SHIELD

In the northeast corner of the province is a remnant of the Canadian Shield, the name given to the mass of hard Precambrian rock which covers much of the country. The region is characterized by marshy depressions and numerous lakes owing to a disorganized drainage system, and Jack Pine is the only species which exists in any abundance.

**Natural Regions**

- Boreal Forest
- Parkland
- Grassland
- Rocky Mountains
- Montane
- Canadian Shield

100 kilometres

Bistcho Lake

Hay River

Slave River

High Level

Peace River

Fort Chipewyan

Lake Claire

Lake Athabasca

Wabasca River

River

Fort McMurray

Peace River

Peace River

Lesser Slave Lake

Athabasca River

Grande Prairie

Smoky

Whitecourt

Athabasca

St. Paul

North Saskatchewan R.

Jasper

Edmonton

Vegreville

Lloydminster

Wetaskiwin

Hocky Mountain House

Stettler

Provost

Red Deer

Banff

Drumheller

Calgary

Red Deer River

Oyen

Bow River

Brooks

South Saskatchewan R.

Oldman River

Medicine Hat

Lethbridge

Milk R.

# ALBERTA ANIMALS

Alberta is home to a vast array of animals, each adapted to exploit a specific environment. The way in which different classes of animals evolved from each other is illustrative of how species within each class are continually evolving to exploit new environments.

## THE FISHES — CLASS OSTEICHTYES

The first fish-like creatures originated in the late Silurian period about 400 million years ago. The group flourished during the Devonian — also known as the Age of Fishes — and dominated the seas for the rest of the Paleozoic era. Today bony fishes are the dominant vertebrates in fresh and salt water, accounting for more than 25,000 species worldwide.

## THE AMPHIBIANS — CLASS AMPHIBIA

The first limbed land dwellers, amphibians evolved from fishes in the Devonian period about 340 million years ago. The major evolutionary advance they made over their ancestors, the lobe-finned fishes, was their ability to free themselves from total dependence on an aquatic environment. By evolving lungs and legs, they became able to exploit rich new habitats on land. The group quickly diversified, and remained dominant on land for over 100 million years.

In addition to the development of lungs and legs, amphibians also evolved a more efficient circulatory system than fish and a heart with three chambers instead of two. Frogs and toads also developed external eardrums to enhance their listening ability, an essential adaptation for surviving on land.

## THE REPTILES — CLASS REPTILIA

Reptiles evolved from amphibian ancestors during the Carboniferous period about 320 million years ago. Unlike their predecessors, they laid shelled eggs and were completely terrestrial. By the start of the Mesozoic era 225 million years ago, reptiles dominated the earth, and continued to rule the land, sea, and air for the next 130 million years. At the end of that era, reptiles mysteriously underwent a mass extinction. The only groups surviving to the present day include turtles, tuatara (an iguanalike creature found in New Zealand), snakes, lizards, and crocodilians.

Reptiles evolved several other characteristics which make them better suited than amphibians for life on land. Their dry skin prevented water loss and protected them from enemies.Fertilization became internal and the young did not undergo a larval stage. The ability to lay shelled eggs or bear live young freed them from dependence on a watery medium for reproduction. They also developed more advanced circulatory and respiratory systems and could move better on land.

## THE BIRDS — CLASS AVES

Birds evolved from reptiles during the Jurassic period in two lineages: the giant pterosaurs which died out with the dinosaurs and the line that gave rise to modern birds.

In addition to wings and feathers, birds evolved a host of adaptations beyond reptiles. Like mammals, they are homeothermic, have an efficient four-chambered heart, and are insulated against the weather. They have well-developed brains, keen senses, and complex behavioural and communicative patterns. Adaptations for flight include hollow bones and an enhanced breathing capacity.

## THE MAMMALS - CLASS MAMMALIA

Mammals evolved during the Triassic and Jurassic periods, and rapidly began to exploit habitats left vacant by reptiles and amphibians. Being warm-blooded, they were more active than other species and able to inhabit colder areas, hunt prey more easily, and avoid predation better than their competition. They underwent a great adaptive radiation in the Mesozoic, and for the past 65 million years they have been the dominant life form on earth. Man is a relatively new addition to the group, having a lineage less than three million years old.

In addition to being warm-blooded, mammals also evolved a different reproductive strategy. Fertilization is internal as in birds and reptiles, but embryonic development occurs in the female's uterus. After birth, the young are fed and nurtured by adults, and during this time they acquire behavioural lessons from their elders and siblings.

# GEOLOGICAL TIME SCALE

| ERA | PERIOD | YEARS AGO | EVENTS |
|---|---|---|---|
| C E N O Z O I C | HOLOCENE | 10,000 | -dominance of man |
| | QUATERNARY | 2.5 MILLION | -first human civilizations |
| | TERTIARY | 65 MILLION | -mammals, birds and insects dominate the land<br>-angiosperms are the dominant land plant |
| M E S O Z O I C | CRETACEOUS | 135 MILLION | -dinosaurs become extinct<br>-mammals undergo great adaptive radiation<br>-great expansion of angiosperms; gymnosperms decline |
| | JURASSIC | 190 MILLION | -Age of Reptiles; dinosaurs abundant<br>-first birds appear |
| | TRIASSIC | 225 MILLION | -first dinosaurs and mammals appear<br>-gymnosperms are the dominant land plant |
| P A L E O Z O I C | PERMIAN | 280 MILLION | -great expansion of reptiles; amphibians decline<br>-many marine invertebrates become extinct |
| | CARBONIFEROUS | 340 MILLION | -Age of Amphibians<br>-first reptiles appear; fish undergo great adaptive radiation |
| | DEVONIAN | 400 MILLION | -Age of Fishes<br>-first amphibians, insects and gymnosperms appear |
| | SILURIAN | 430 MILLION | -first jawed fish appear<br>-plants move onto land |
| | ORDOVICIAN | 500 MILLION | -first vertebrates appear |
| | CAMBRIAN | 600 MILLION | -marine invertebrates and algae abundant |

# ALBERTA MAMMALS

Mammals are warm-blooded, animals which possess milk-producing mammary glands. Most mammals are covered in hair, an adaptation which helps to prevent loss of body heat to the environment, have four feet and a tail and have several different kinds of teeth. Other physiological characteristics include a four-chambered heart, a diaphragm to increase breathing efficiency, and sweat glands. Mammals have three bones in the middle ear to enhance hearing (birds and reptiles have one).

## HOW TO IDENTIFY MAMMALS

Mammals are generally wary of humans and are difficult to spot in the field. However, groups like rodents, rabbits, dogs, bears and big game species like elk and deer are commonly encountered if one knows where to look for them.

Since many mammals are wary of predators, some of the best places to look for them are in undisturbed areas affording some source of cover including woods and wood edges, swamps, thickets, and rural fields and meadows.

When you spot a mammal, consider its size, shape, and colour. Check for distinguishing field marks which can help you place it within its family. Consult the text descriptions to confirm your sighting.

Below are examples of tracks of a few Alberta mammals. For more information see *Animal Tracks of Western Canada* by Joanne Barwise or The Peterson *Field Guide to Animal Tracks*.

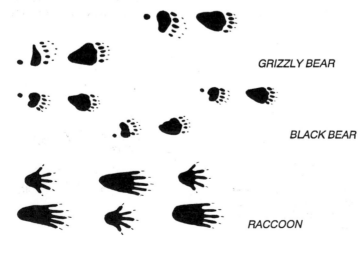

GRIZZLY BEAR

BLACK BEAR

RACCOON

## INSECTIVORES

This group of insect-eating animals includes the moles and shrews. All have pointed snouts, sharp teeth, and clawed feet.

### MASKED SHREW
*Sorex cinereus*
10 cm (4 in.)

A common insectivore found in moist habitats throughout the province. Distinguished by its small size, brown coat, pointed nose, and beady eyes. Highly active, it often eats more than three times its weight each day in insects. Primarily nocturnal. Their presence can sometimes be detected by the small tunnels they make under leaf litter and vegetation. One of five Alberta shrew species.

## BATS

The only true flying mammals, bats are common throughout Alberta. Primarily nocturnal, they have developed a sophisticated sonar system, echolocation, to help them hunt at night. As they fly, they emit a series of high frequency sounds that bounce back off objects in their path. Based on the characteristics of the returning soundwaves, bats are able to determine what objects or prey lie in their path. Most feed primarily on insects. During daylight, they seek refuge in caves, trees and attics. Bats are rarely harmful and are valuable in helping to check insect populations. Of the eight species found in Alberta, the following two are widely distributed.

### LITTLE BROWN BAT
*Myotis lucifugus*
9 cm (3.5 in.)

Found throughout the province in a variety of habitats from forests and fields to city parks. The most common bat in Alberta, it is identified by its small size and glossy coat which is dark brown above, buffy below. Most active at dawn and dusk, it is sometimes spotted feeding during the day. Hibernates during winter.

### BIG BROWN BAT
*Eptesicus fuscus*
12 cm (4.7 in.)

Found in wooded and open areas throughout the province. Told from the Little Brown Bat by its larger size, and pale to dark brown coat. An erratic flier, it often hawks for insects near treetops or street lamps at dusk. It is the commonest rabies carrier among bats and often hibernates in buildings during winter.

## PIKAS

Close relatives of rabbits. Pikas inhabit rockslides in the mountains. Active during the day, they can often be seen foraging for grasses and herbs.

### ROCKY MOUNTAIN PIKA
*Ocohotona princeps*
19 cm (7.5 in.)

Common near rockslides at high elevations in the mountain region. Distinguished by the rounded body, large ears, and lack of a tail. Active throughout the year, it spends the majority of the warmer months gathering food for winter. Pikas have the unusual habit of drying harvested vegetation in the sun (like hay) before storing it.

# HARES AND RABBITS

Members of this distinctive group of mammals have long ears, large eyes, and long hind legs. Primarily nocturnal, they commonly rest in protected areas like thickets during the day. When threatened, they often thump their hind feet on the ground as an alarm signal. Hares and jackrabbits are distinguished from cottontails and rabbits in two ways: the former are generally larger, and they give birth to precocial (active), rather than altricial (helpless), young. ·

## NUTTALL'S COTTONTAIL
*Sylvilagus nuttalli*
36 cm (14 in.)

Found in open forests and shrubby areas. The smallest rabbit-eared animal in Alberta, it is distinguished by its gray-brown coat, unmarked ears, and hairy hind feet. Feeds primarily on grass. Most active at dawn and dusk. Rests in thickets during the day.

## SNOWSHOE HARE
*Lepus americanus*
45 cm (18 in.)

Common in forests and brushy areas near swamps. Key field marks are its large hind feet and black-tipped ears. Feet are heavily furred to allow travel over deep snow. Coat is white in winter, brown in summer. Most active at dawn and dusk.

## WHITE-TAILED PRAIRIE HARE
*Lepus townsendii*
61 cm (24 in.)

Also known as the White-tailed Jack Rabbit, it is commonly found on open prairies and fields. Distinguished by its large size, long hind legs, black-tipped ears, and white tail. Coat is gray in summer, whitish in winter. Highly athletic, it is capable of reaching speeds of 65 kph (40 mph). Most active at dawn and dusk.

## SQUIRRELS

This diverse family of hairy-tailed, large-eyed rodents includes chipmunks, tree squirrels, ground squirrels, and marmots. All but the tree squirrels live in burrows throughout the year. Most are active during the day.

### LEAST CHIPMUNK
*Eutamias minimus* 18 cm (7 in.)
### YELLOW PINE CHIPMUNK
*Eutamias amoenus* 20 cm (8 in.)

Common in coniferous forests. Least Chipmunk (left) is smaller size, with facial stripes, and long back stripes to the base of the tail. Note tawny ears and long tail. Large expandable cheek pouches are used to gather food. Hibernates in winter. Has a high-pitched, chipping call. The Yellow Pine Chipmunk (right) is told from the Least Chipmunk by the black on the front of its ears and pronounced body stripes. Found only in the mountains and foothills
|||||||||| distribution area of Yellow Pine Chipmunk

### RED SQUIRREL
*Tamiasciurus hudsonicus*
32 cm (12.5 in.)

Abundant in coniferous and mixed woods, it also thrives in urban areas. Coat is rusty red-black above, white below. Note large, bushy tail. Calls include chatters, grunts, and clicks. It spends the winter in ground burrows and uses tree nests the rest of the year. Feeds largely on conifer seeds which it harvests throughout the year.

### EASTERN GRAY SQUIRREL
*Sciurus carolinensis*
45 cm (18 in.)

This introduced tree squirrel is very common in the urban area of Calgary and is distinguished by its large size and gray or black coat. It lives in deciduous trees and is most active in the early morning and late afternoon.

## NORTHERN FLYING SQUIRREL
*Glaucomys sabrinus*
28 cm (11 in.)

Found in mixed and coniferous forests, this is the only nocturnal squirrel in the province. Distinguished by its gray-brown coat, white undersides, and the loose fold of skin between its front and hind legs. By stretching this loose skin taut, it can glide between trees for distances of up to 40 metres (130 ft.).

## WOODCHUCK
*Marmota monax*
60 cm (24 in.)

A solitary mammal found in fields, open woods, and brushy areas in central and northern Alberta. Also referred to as a Ground Hog, it is distinguished by its chunky profile, frosted brown coat, and dark feet. A true hibernator, it sleeps undisturbed during its winter dormancy of 4-6 months. In Alberta, it usually ends its hibernation long after the celebrated Ground Hog's Day on February 2.

## HOARY MARMOT
*Marmota caligata*
70 cm (28 in.)

Commonly found in high alpine meadows near rockslides. A heavy-bodied rodent, it is told by its silvery fur, black feet, and black head and shoulder patches. Lives in small colonies. Nicknamed "Whistler" for its shrill alarm call, it hibernates for up to 8 months a year. Its less common cousin, the Yellow-bellied Marmot (*Marmota flaviventris* ), is found in southern Rockies.

# GROUND SQUIRRELS

These ground-dwelling rodents are widespread throughout central and southern Alberta. Stricly diurnal in activity, they are easily observed feeding in open areas, and running in and out of their multi-chambered tunnels. All have expandable cheek pouches to carry quantities of food to their burrows. Most populations are large and highly successful. All hibernate in winter. Feed primarily on seeds, insects, and vegetation.

## THIRTEEN-LINED GROUND SQUIRREL
*Spermophilus tridecemlineatus*
22 cm (8.5 in.)

A small ground squirrel common to open fields and grasslands in southern Alberta. The unique lined pattern along back and sides is unmistakable. Underground burrows lack mounds of telltale dirt near their entrance. Diet consists largely of insects and weed seeds.

## RICHARDSON'S GROUND SQUIRREL
*Spermophilus richardsonii*
30 cm (12 in.)

Very common in fields and pastures. It's hard not to spot one when driving in rural southern Alberta. Coat is yellow-gray above and light below. Feeds on green vegetation, seeds, meat, and insects. Found in large colonies.

## COLUMBIAN GROUND SQUIRREL
*Spermophilus columbianus*
36 cm (14 in.)

Common in alpine grasslands and meadows, this is the largest ground squirrel found in the province. Told at a glance by its gray back and rusty legs and belly. Hibernates 7-8 months of the year (August-March). Eats a higher proportion of meat and insects than other ground squirrels.

## GOLDEN-MANTLED GROUND SQUIRREL
*Spermophilus lateralis*
25 cm (10 in.)

This large chipmunk-coloured squirrel is found in rocky areas in the mountain region. Easily distinguished by its rusty head and long side stripes. Unlike chipmunks, it lacks a facial stripe across its eye. A solitary mammal, it often, however, joins in groups to accept handouts from hikers.

## POCKET GOPHERS

This family of burrowing mammals are named for their fur-lined, external cheek pouches which are used to carry food to storage. Though rarely seen above ground, their presence can be detected by the numerous small mounds of earth they push up while digging their tunnels.

## NORTHERN POCKET GOPHER
*Thomomys talpoides*
20 cm (8 in.)

Common in fields, meadows, and open forests throughout southern and central Alberta. Gray-brown in colour, it has small, bead-like eyes, small ears, and large front claws and its incisor teeth are always exposed. Feeds primarily on tubers, roots, and vegetation.

## BEAVER

The single representative of this family is found in abundance throughout the province.

### BEAVER
*Castor canadensis*
71 cm (37 in.)

This large rodent is found in wooded ponds, streams, and lakes throughout Alberta. Key field marks are a glossy brown coat, exposed incisor teeth, and a large, flattened, black tail. When threat-ened, it slaps its tail on the water as a warning signal. Eats primarily bark and twigs, favouring aspen, birch and poplar trees. Largely nocturnal, it can often be seen skimming across the water at dusk. Typically, families live in large conical dams constructed from sticks and mud.

## MICE & ALLIES

Members of this family of rodents are widely distibuted throughout the province. Tails are typically covered with short hairs. Most live on the ground.

### SOUTHERN BOREAL RED-BACKED VOLE
*Clethrionomys gapperi*
14 cm (5.5 in.)

Common in damp woodlands with dense ground cover. Coat is typically gray-brown above with a wide rusty band down the middle of the back and silvery below. Gray phase also occurs which lacks a rusty stripe. Feeds on vegetation, seeds, and berries. Active year-round, it can often be detected by the small tunnels it makes in the grass or snow. One of eight Alberta vole species.

## HOUSE MOUSE
*Mus musculus*
13 cm (5 in.)

This familiar mouse is the most common rodent in Alberta and is found near human dwellings. Told by its gray coat, large eyes and ears, and scaly tail. Normally lives in colonies. Females have up to 14 litters of 3-16 young annually. Feeds on grains, vegetables and refuse. Originally introduced from Europe. Albino strains of each species are widely used for laboratory experimentation.

## DEER MOUSE
*Peromyscus maniculatus*
17 cm (6.5 in.)

Common and widespread throughout the province in a variety of habitats. Distinguished by its bicoloured coat which is tan above and white below. The hairy tail is also bicoloured and nearly as long as the body. Young have gray coats. Feeds on seeds, buds, berries and insects and is active year round.

## BUSHY-TAILED WOODRAT
*Neotoma cinerea*
36 cm (14 in.)

The only rat native to Canada, the woodrat is found in forests and along rocky alpine slopes. It is distinguished by its large eyes and ears, long coat, and bushy tail. Usually nests along cliffs, which it stains white and yellow with urine and feces. Feeds primarily on vegetation and seeds. Also called a packrat, it often hoards shiny objects which it steals from campers and hikers.

## MUSKRAT
*Ondatra zibethicus*
56 cm (22 in.)

This aquatic rodent is found in marshes, ponds, and reedy lakes. Key field marks are its glossy brown coat, silvery belly, and scaly, laterally flattened, black tail. Muskrats commonly live in conical, island-like lodges of vegetation, up to 1 m (3 ft.) above water. Highly active at dawn and dusk, muskrats feed on vegetation and small aquatic animals.

## JUMPING MICE

These mice have a long tail and large hind legs which help them to travel "kangaroo style" in great leaps. Found in woodlands, swamps and meadows, they lead a secretive, nocturnal existence.

## WESTERN JUMPING MOUSE
*Zapus princeps*
23 cm (9 in.)

Found near streams and marshes in moist meadows and open woodlands. Of the three subspecies of jumping mice found in Alberta, the most common lives in the mountains. Coat is olive above, yellow on the sides, and white below. Identified by its large hind feet and a long tail which assist it in bounding across the ground. Capable of leaping up to 2 m (6 ft.). Hibernates from October to May. Primarily nocturnal, it is also active during the day.

# PORCUPINES

Porcupines are small, gray-black, dog-sized creatures with coats of stiff, barbed quills.

## PORCUPINE
*Erethizon dorsatum*
70 cm (28 in.)

Common in forests and shrubby ravines throughout the province. Told at a glance by its chunky profile, arched back, and long gray coat. Body is covered with barbed quills which protect it against most predators. When threatened, it faces away from its aggressor, erects its quills, and lashes out with its heavily armed tail: the loosely rooted quills detach on contact. Primarily nocturnal, its diet consists of leaves, twigs, and bark. Sluggish on land, porcupines spend much of their time in trees.

# WEASELS & ALLIES

Members of this group usually have small heads, long necks, short legs, and long bodies. All have prominent anal scent glands which are used for social and sexual communication. Primarily nocturnal, they feed largely on small mammals. (For proper classification, see p.178.)

## ERMINE
*Mustela erminea*
33 cm (13 in.)

The Ermine, or Short-tailed Weasel, is found in open wooded areas and farmlands, usually near water. Field marks include slender body, long neck, and black-tipped short tail. Summer coat is brown above, white below. Winter coat is all white except for black tip on tail. A nocturnal hunter, it is a fearless, aggressive killer.

### LONG-TAILED WEASEL
*Mustela frenata*
47 cm (18.5 in.)

Found near water in open woodlands, meadows, and fields. Distinguished from the Ermine in summer by its larger size, longer tail and brown feet. Winter coat is identical to the Ermine's. Weasels are aggressive hunters which kill their prey with a bite to the base of the neck. Noted for their ferocity, they will occasionally go on killing sprees and take far more prey than they can immediately consume, often storing the meat for the future.

### MINK
*Mustela vison*
56 cm (22 in.)

These nocturnal animals are common near water in a variety of habitats. Rich brown coats and white chin patches are good field marks. Excellent swimmers, they are able to supplement their diet of small mammals with fish and frogs. Hundreds of thousands are trapped or farmed annually in Canada for their pelts.

### STRIPED SKUNK
*Mephitis mephitis*
61 cm (24 in.)

Common in open wooded areas throughout the province. Told by its black coat, white forehead stripe, and white side stripes. Protects itself when threatened by spraying aggressors with noxious smelling fluid from its anal glands. It can spray this fluid up to 6m (20 ft.). Feeds on vegetation, insects and small animals.

## BADGER
*Taxidea taxus*
76 cm (30 in.)

Found in native grasslands and uncultivated pastures. A squat, heavy-bodied animal, it is identified by its long yellow-gray coat, white forehead stripe, and huge claws. A prodigious burrower, it feeds mostly on ground squirrels and other burrowing mammals. It is the only member of the weasel family to hibernate. Badgers are suffering a serious decline in population owing to a loss of habitat due to farming.

## RACCOON FAMILY

The Raccoon belongs to a family of mammals which includes the Coati of Central and South America and the Lesser Panda of Asia. Some experts also believe the Giant Panda belongs to this group.

## RACCOON
*Procyon lotor*
89 cm (35 in.)

Common in wooded areas near water in the Milk River drainage of southern Alberta. Easily identified by its gray-brown coat, black mask and ringed tail. Feeds on small animals, insects, invertebrates, and refuse. Often dunks its food into water before eating it. Primarily nocturnal, it may be abroad at any time of day.

## DOG-LIKE MAMMALS

Members of this family have long snouts, large ears, and resemble domestic dogs in looks and habit. Active year-round.

### RED FOX
*Vulpes vulpes*
96 cm (38 in.)

This sleek, large-eared animal is found in semi-open country throughout Alberta. Coat is normally red, but black and red-black variants exist. Best field mark is the bushy, white-tipped tail. Primarily nocturnal, it feeds on small mammals, birds, berries and fruit.

### COYOTE
*Canis latrans*
1.2 m (47 in.)

Found in a variety of wooded and open areas throughout the province. Identified by its gray-yellow coat, large ears, pointed nose, and bushy, black-tipped tail. Holds tail down when running. Largely a nocturnal hunter, it is often seen loping across fields at dawn and dusk. Feeds on rodents, rabbits, berries and carrion.

### GRAY WOLF
*Canis lupus*
1.6 m (63 in.)

Found in forested and tundra areas. Coat is normally gray, but variants range from white to black. Similar to the Coyote, the Gray Wolf is larger, has a broader nose pad, and holds its tail high when running. Lives in groups with a complex social hierarchy.

## CAT-LIKE MAMMALS

These highly specialized carnivores are noted for their legendary hunting ability. All have short faces, keen vision, powerful bodies, and retractible claws. Most are nocturnal hunters.

### CANADA LYNX
*Lynx canadensis*
1 m (39 in.)

Found in heavily wooded forests and swamps in the mountains and northern Alberta. Distinguished by its long coat, tufted ears, and short, black-tipped tail. Its large, thickly-furred feet are adapted for travelling over the snow. This nocturnal hunter feeds largely on Snowshoe Hare and some smaller mammals. Its rare southern cousin, the Bobcat, looks similar to the Lynx but has a tail which is black only on the upper side.

### MOUNTAIN LION
*Felis concolor*
2 m (78 in.)

Also referred to as the cougar or puma, it inhabits remote forests and swamps in the mountains and foothills. Field marks include tan coat, white belly, and long tail. A solitary hunter, it feeds largely on cloven-hoofed mammals, hares and other small mammals. Regarded as an endangered species.

# BEARS

This group includes the largest terrestrial carnivores in the world. All are heavy-bodied, large-headed animals, with short ears and small tails. Their sense of smell is keen, though eyesight is generally poor. Diet consists of berries, vegetation, fish, insects, mammals, and refuse. Though Alberta's bears hibernate during winter, they are not considered true hibernators since they will often rise to go out of their dens during warm spells. Young are born in January-February.

## BLACK BEAR
*Ursus americanus*
1.7 m (66 in.)

 The most common bear in the province, it is found in forested and swampy areas. Coat is normally black, but cinnamon variants also occur. Note straight profile of snout. Diet consists largely of vegetation, berries, carrion, and fish.

## GRIZZLY BEAR
*Ursus arctos*
2 m (78 in.)

 Found in isolated mountain meadows and tundra areas, grizzlies normally inhabit higher terrain than black bears. Best field marks are large shoulder hump and dished face. Long coat has frosted appearance. Primarily nocturnal, they feed on vegetation, fish, insects, and both large and small mammals. Often cache uneaten game. Once common, these bears are currently regarded as a threatened species.

# DEER & ALLIES

This group includes many popular big game species including deer, moose, and elk. Males of each species possess "true" antlers which are shed annually. Each year the antlers grow anew under a coating of "velvet" rich in blood vessels. When the antlers are fully grown -shortly before mating season- the velvet is shed. A few months after mating season the antlers are also shed.

## WHITE-TAILED DEER
*Odocoileus virginianus*
2 m (80 in.)

 Common in forests, farmlands, and river valleys. Named for its large, white-edged tail which is held aloft (flag-like) when running. Coat is tan in summer, gray in winter. An agile, elusive deer, it can reach speeds of 65 kph (40 mph) and leap obstacles as high as 2.5 m (8 ft.). Most active at dawn and dusk.

## MULE DEER
*Odocoileus hemionus*
2 m (80 in.)

 Found in open forests and wooded river valleys. Coat is tan in summer, gray in winter. Key field marks are large ears and black-tipped tail. Feeds mostly on shrubs, twigs, and grasses. Males shed horns between January-March. Essentially a solitary species, mule deer often form herds during mating season and winter.

## ELK
*Cervus elaphus*
2.4 m (94 in.)

Also called Wapiti, the elk is common in open forests and meadows in the mountains and foothills. Distinguished by its large size, shaggy dark neck, and light rump patch. Most active at dawn and dusk, it feeds on grass, lichen, and twigs. Elk usually travel in herds. Males shed antlers February-April.

### MOOSE
*Alces alces*
2.7 m (106")

Commonly found in swamp and forest areas in the mountains, foothills, and northern Alberta. The largest member of its family, the horse-sized moose is easily indentified by its long thin legs and overhanging snout. Males also possess enormous, flattened antlers, and a prominent neck "bell" of skin and hair. Largely solitary animals, they are most active at dawn and dusk.

## PRONGHORN

This family which dates back over 20 million years ago contains a single surviving species. Pronghorns are small, deer-like ungulates with short tails, long ears and simple pronged horns.

### PRONGHORN
*Antilocapra americana*
1.4 m (55 in.)

Found on grasslands in extreme southern Alberta, it is identified by its white throat bands, and white rump patch. Both sexes possess unique horns consisting of a bony core covered by a hardened sheath of hairs. Only the sheath is shed annually. Extremely agile, the Pronghorn can reach speeds up to 65 kph (40 mph). Active during the day.

## SHEEP, GOATS AND CATTLE

Members of both sexes in this family possess unbranched horns which are never shed. Domestic cattle, sheep, and goats also belong to this group.

### BIGHORN SHEEP
*Ovis canadensis*
1.7 m (68 in.)

Found in the mountain and foothills, along rugged slopes and meadows. A stocky, gray-brown animal, it is easily told by its huge coiled horns. A powerful climber, it has specialized hooves which enhance traction on the rocky slopes. Males and females form separate herds for most of the year.

### MOUNTAIN GOAT
*Oreamnos americanus*
1.8 m (71 in.)

Found high in the mountains on rocky slopes, usually above treeline. Identified by its long, shaggy white coat and pointed black horns. Coat is shed in late summer. Like the Bighorn Sheep, the Mountain Goat possesses specialized hooves which enhance traction on mountainsides. Most active at dawn and dusk.

### BISON
*Bison bison*
3.4 m (134 in.)

Once numbering in the tens of millions, bison are now found only on reserves. Two subspecies are protected in the province. Herds of the larger, woollier Wood Bison are found in Banff and Wood Buffalo National Parks. Plains Bison inhabit Waterton and Elk Island National Parks. Bison are easily recognized by the shaggy head and shoulders and large shoulder hump.

# ALBERTA BIRDS

Birds are feathered animals with wings. The majority can fly, and those that cannot are believed to have descended from ancestors that did.

Like reptiles, birds are fertilized internally and lay eggs. Their eggs are different, however, having hard rather than leathery shells. The eggs are normally incubated by the male or female parents, though some parasitic species like the Brown-headed Cowbird lay their eggs in the nests of other birds. After the young are hatched, they are nurtured for a period of up to several weeks until they are able to fly.

How to identify birds

As with other species, the best way to become good at identifying birds is simply by practice. The more birds you attempt to identify, the better you'll become at distinguishing species.

When birdwatching, the first thing to note is the habitat you are exploring, in order to know what kinds of birds to expect: ducks are found in marshes, herons on shorelines, and woodpeckers in woods. You won't find a grouse on the water or a loon up a tree. When you spot a bird, try and determine its size and shape. Is it small (sparrow-sized), medium (robin-sized), or large (crow-sized)? Is it slender like a vireo, or chunky like a chickadee? Note the shape of its beak. Look at the colour and pattern of its feathers for any distinguishing markings. Does it have any unusual behavioural characteristics? Listen to its voice and try to distinguish a pattern in its song. When you've got a good mental picture of what it looks like, compare it to the illustrations. Consult the text to confirm your sighting.

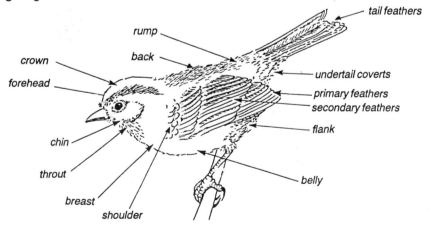

The silhouettes on this page are included to help you in identifying certain types of birds in flight. An illustration of a diving duck running along the water as it takes off is also included.

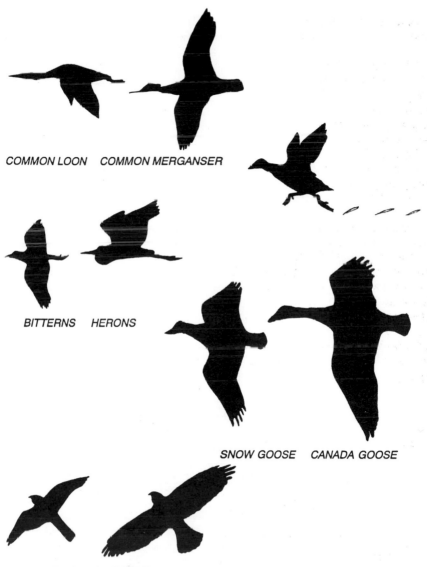

COMMON LOON    COMMON MERGANSER

BITTERNS    HERONS

SNOW GOOSE    CANADA GOOSE

FALCONS    HAWKS

## LOONS

These torpedo-shaped diving birds are commonly found on isolated stretches of water on lakes and large rivers. Excellent swimmers, they can dive to depths of 60 m (200 ft.). Loons have the ability to submerge most of their body and swim about with only their heads above water. Sexes are similar in appearance.

### COMMON LOON
*Gavia immer*
76 cm (30 in.)

Found on wooded ponds and lakes, it is best known for its haunting call that echoes across the water at night. Distinguished in summer by its black head and black-and-white checkered back. Note stout, straight bill. Winter plumage is gray and white. Feeds primarily on fish. Night call is a resonant *ha-oo, ha-oo-oo*. (April-October)

*winter*

*summer*

## GREBES

The members of this group of duck-like birds have short tails, slender necks, and stiff, pointed bills (excluding the Pied-billed Grebe). Excellent divers, they have lobed toes rather than webbed feet, and their legs are located near the back of the body to provide better propulsion through the water. Weak fliers, they need to taxi across the water's surface before becoming airborne. Like loons, they are able to submerge their body at will. They are noted for their elaborate dancing courtship rituals. Diet consists of crustaceans, insects, and small aquatic animals.

### PIED-BILLED GREBE
*Podilymbus podiceps*
30 cm (12 in.)

A small, solitary bird found on weed-choked marshes and ponds. Identified in summer by its dark neck and black-banded, chicken-like bill. Adults in non-breeding plumage and young lack black marks on their bill. (May-September)

*winter*

*summer*

## EARED GREBE
*Podiceps nigricollis*
33 cm (13 in.)

Found in colonies on shallow sloughs and lakes. Distinguished in summer by its crested black head, black throat and neck, and golden ear tufts. Slender bill appears upturned when swimming. Non-breeding adults have grayish-white necks and white ear and throat patches. (April-September)

*winter*

*summer*

## HORNED GREBE
*Podiceps auritus*
33 cm (13 in.)

This small bird is mainly found on shallow ponds and sloughs. Similar to the Eared Grebe, it is distinguished by its uncrested black head, reddish neck, and prominent golden ear tufts. Non-breeding adults are dark above with a white chin and neck. Does not nest in colonies. (April-October)

*winter*

*summer*

## RED-NECKED GREBE
*Podiceps grisegena*
48 cm (19 in.)

This large grebe is one of the commonest diving birds on Alberta lakes. Distinguished in summer by its long rusty neck, white cheeks and yellow bill. Non-breeding adults develop distinctive white crescents on their gray heads. (April-October)

*winter*

*summer*

# BITTERNS & HERONS

This group is composed of large wading birds with long legs, long necks, and slender bills. Most inhabit marshes and other shallows where they feed on fish, frogs, and insects. Sexes similar. All fly with their necks folded into an 'S' curve. For taxonomic classification, see *Checklists* in back.

## AMERICAN BITTERN
*Botaurus lentiginosus*
71 cm (28 in.)

This elusive marsh bird often skulks in and around the reedy margins of sloughs and lakes. Black neck marks and a heavily streaked breast are key field marks. Blackish outer edge of wing is evident in flight. If approached, the bittern often attempts to avoid detection by extending its neck and bill skyward and freezing. Most active late in the day. Though hard to spot, its song, resembling a rusty water pump, is distinctive. (May-October)

## GREAT BLUE HERON
*Ardea herodias*
1 m (40 in.)

A large gray-blue bird found on the borders of rivers, streams, and lakes. Distinguished in the field by its large size, long legs, long bill, and whitish face. Note the black plumes extending back from the eye. Often seen stalking fish and frogs in still waters. (April-October)

# GEESE

Geese are large, long-necked birds found near ponds and marshes throughout Alberta. Highly terrestrial, they are often spotted grazing in fields and meadows. Their diet consists largely of grasses, grains, and some aquatic plants. Noisy in flight, they are often heard before being seen when passing overhead.

## CANADA GOOSE
*Branta canadensis*
60-100 cm (24-40 in.)

Found near marshes, ponds, lakes, and rivers throughout Alberta. The most common goose in North America, it is easily identified by its black head and neck and prominent white cheek patch. Ten subspecies have been identified which differ mainly in size. Geese fly in a 'V' formation when migrating. Pairs mate for life. Call is a nasal *honk*. (April-November; some overwinter in southern Alberta)

## SNOW GOOSE
*Chen caerulescens*
70 cm (27 in.)

A common migrant, the Snow Goose frequents marshes, sloughs, and shallow lakes. Adults are typically white with black wing tips. Dark variants — called Blue Geese — also exist which have a white head and a dark blue body. Note distinctive bill shape. Young birds have gray backs and white underparts. Flocks may number over 10,000. (April-May; September-October)

≋ only during migration

## DUCKS

Smaller than geese, ducks have shorter necks and are much more aquatic. They are divided into four groups: surface-feeding ducks, which feed by tipping over and pulling up vegetation; diving ducks, which dive for their food and have to run along the water to take off; fish-eating birds, which also dive and have toothed beaks; and stiff-tailed ducks, which have a stiff tail and are almost helpless on land.

SURFACE-FEEDING DUCKS

### GREEN-WINGED TEAL
*Anas crecca*
36 cm (14 in.)

The smallest duck in the province, it is found in shallow lakes and ponds. The breeding male is told by its brown head, glossy green face patch, and vertical white wing bar. The female is distinguished from similar species by her short bill and unmarked forewing. Speculum is green. (April-October)

*male*        *female*

### BLUE-WINGED TEAL
*Anas discors*
38 cm (15 in.)

A small duck often found in mixed flocks on marshes and ponds. The male is distinguished by its white facial crescent and white patch near its tail. The female is a mottled brown. Both sexes have a blue wing patch and a green speculum. (April-September)

*female*

*male*

## AMERICAN WIGEON
*Anas americana*
50 cm (20 in.)

Though primarily aquatic, these ducks can often be found nibbling grass on the shores of ponds and marshes . Male is brownish with white flanks, a white forehead, and a glossy green face patch. Female is told by her bluish bill and flecked head. Speculum is green. (April-October)

*male*

*female*

## NORTHERN SHOVELER
*Anas clypeata*
50 cm (20 in.)

Frequently found on ponds and sloughs. Distinctive shovel-shaped bill is used to strain aquatic animals from the water. Also feeds on vegetation. Male has a green head, rusty sides, and a blue wing patch. Female is distinguished from other brown ducks by her large bill. Both sexes swim with bill pointed downward. Green speculum is duller in the female. (May-October)

*female*

*male*

## GADWALL
*Anas strepera*
50 cm (20 in.)

Unlike most dabbling ducks, gadwalls often dive for food. The gray male has a mottled brown head and is distinguished by its white wing patch and black rear. The female is mottled brown with a yellow bill. Both sexes have a white speculum and yellow feet. Essentially solitary birds, they are occasionally seen in flocks with other surface feeders. (April-September)

*male*

*female*

## MALLARD
*Anas platyrhynchos*
58 cm (23 in.)

The ancestor of domestic ducks, the Mallard is abundant on ponds and marshes throughout the province. The male is identified by its green head, white collar and chestnut breast. The female is mottled brown. Both have a metallic blue speculum. Call is a loud quack. (March-November; large numbers often overwinter in Calgary, Galahad, and Wabamun)

*male*                    *female*

## NORTHERN PINTAIL
*Anas acuta*
66 cm (26 in.)

The most widespread duck in Canada, the Northern Pintail is found on shallow marshes and ponds. Distinguished at a glance by its long neck and pointed tail, the brown-headed male has a white breast and a white neck stripe. The female has a more pointed tail than similar species. Glossy brown speculum is bordered in white. (April-October)

*female*

*male*

DIVING DUCKS

## BUFFLEHEAD
*Bucephala albeola*
36 cm (14 in.)

A small, puffy-headed duck found on wooded ponds and rivers during nesting season. Male is told by the large white patch on its iridescent black head. Female is gray-black and has a small white cheek patch. The Bufflehead is the only diving duck able to take off from the water without running along its surface. (April-November; some overwinter in southern Alberta)

*female*

*male*

## LESSER SCAUP
*Aythya affinis*
40 cm (16 in.)

A true diving duck, it is found on deep ponds and lakes. Male distinguished from Ring-necked Duck by its light back and greenish head. Female has a distinctive white patch at base of bill. Both sexes display a broad white band on the trailing edge of the wing in flight. (April-October)

*male*

*female*

## RING-NECKED DUCK
*Aythya collaris*
43 cm (17 in.)

Common on wooded ponds, lakes, and bogs. Male is distinguished by its white-ringed bill, light gray flanks, and vertical white side stripe. Brown female has light eye rings and a white bill ring. (April-October)

*male*

*female*

## HARLEQUIN DUCK
*Histrionicus histrionicus*
43 cm (17 in.)

Found on mountain streams and lakes. Male's blue-gray plumage is unmistakable. Brownish female has three white facial spots and unmarked wings. (May-September)

*female*

*male*

### COMMON GOLDENEYE
*Bucephala clangula*
48 cm (19 in.)

Found on wooded lakes and ponds during nesting season. Male is identified by a round white spot between its eye and bill. Female has a brown head and an incomplete white neck ring. Wings whistle loudly in flight. (March-October; some overwinter in southern Alberta)

male

female

### REDHEAD
*Aythya americana*
53 cm (21 in.)

A familiar bird that often congregates with other ducks on lakes and ponds. Gray male has a round, rusty head, black breast, and white underparts. Note black-tipped blue bill. Female is brownish with a dull white patch near the base of her bill. (April-October)

male

female

### CANVASBACK
*Aythya valisineria*
53 cm (21 in.)

Found on deep lakes and marshes. Note sloping profile of head. Light gray male has rusty head and neck, and a black breast. Red-headed female is duller and lacks a black breast. Breeds throughout the province. (April-October)

female

male

## WHITE-WINGED SCOTER
*Melanitta fusca*
53 cm (21 in.)

Plump, thick-necked birds found in flocks on deep lakes and large rivers. Black male is told by its swollen bill and white wing and eye patches. Drab females have white wing patches and two light facial patches. (April-September)

*male*

*female*

FISH-EATING DUCKS

## COMMON MERGANSER
*Mergus merganser*
64 cm (25 in.)

This large fish-eating duck is commonly found on wooded lakes and rivers. Note the sleek profile and the long slender bill. The male is told by its iridescent black-green head and white underparts. Female has a crested rufous head and a sharply defined white throat. (April-October). Its less common cousin, the Red-breasted Merganser, breeds in northern Alberta.

*male*

*female*

STIFF-TAILED DUCKS

## RUDDY DUCKS
*Oxyura jamaicensis*
41 cm (16 in.)

Found on ponds, lakes, and sloughs, the Ruddy Duck belongs to a separate subfamily of stiff-tailed ducks. Both sexes are distinguished during nesting season by their chunky bodies, white cheeks, and uplifted tails. Males also have prominent blue beaks. Like loons, they can submerge at will and sometimes swim about with only their heads above water. (May-September)

*female*

*male*

## COOTS

Coots are chicken-like birds often found in the company of ducks and geese in marshes. They rarely fly far, except on migration. Diet consists of aquatic plants, insects, seeds,buds and crustaceans. For classification see p.175.

### AMERICAN COOT
*Fulica americana*
38 cm (15 in.)

Found on ponds, marshes and sloughs. Though the coot belongs to a different order from the rest of the ducks, it is duck-like enough in habit to be included here. Best field marks are its chicken-like white bill, white rear, long green legs, and lobed toes. Feeds on the shore and in the water. Habitually pumps its head back and forth when swimming. (April-September)

## HAWKS

Primarily carnivorous, these birds have sharp talons for grasping prey, and sharply hooked bills for tearing into flesh. The Red-tailed and Swainson's Hawks have large, broad wings and a fan-shaped tail and soar on wind currents when hunting. The smaller Northern Harrier has slim wings and is a low, gliding hunter. Sexes are similar in most species, though females are larger.

### NORTHERN HARRIER
*Circus cyaneus*
50 cm (20 in.)

A slim, gliding hawk common in marshes and prairies. Male is pale gray with a white rump. Females and young are streaked brown. Long wings are tilted upwards in flight. Unlike other hawks which scout prey from afar, it hunts by gliding close to the ground and surprising small animals and birds. (April-November)

### SWAINSON'S HAWK
*Buteo swainsoni*
50 cm (20 in.)

Commonly found on prairies, it is often spotted perched close to the ground on fence posts. Identified by its white underparts and dark breast and back when perching. In flight it is distinguished by its finely banded tail, dark breastband, and dark flight feathers (those on the outer edge of the wing). Diet consists mostly of ground squirrels, mice, and grasshoppers. (April-August)

### RED-TAILED HAWK
*Buteo jamaicensis*
56 cm (22 in.)

This familiar hawk is often spotted gliding high over open fields and forests in search of prey. Identified in flight by its streaked breast, unbanded tail, and white flight feathers. Red tail is usually an excellent field mark. (April-September)

## FALCONS

These large-headed birds of prey are built for speed with slender bodies, long, pointed wings and long tails.

### AMERICAN KESTREL
*Falco sparverius*
28 cm (11 in.)

Formerly called the "Sparrow Hawk", it is common and widespread in wooded and open areas throughout the province. Male told by its rusty back and tail, spotted blue wings, and black facial marks. Note long, narrow, pointed wings. Feeds largely on small birds, rodents, and insects. (April-October)

## MERLIN
*Falco columbarius*
56 cm (22 in.)

Found in woodlands and open areas. Male is blue-gray above, streaked brown below, and has a heavily banded tail. Females and young are similar but are dark brown above. Wings are similar to American Kestrel's but shorter. Both belong to the falcon family.

## CHICKEN-LIKE BIRDS

These ground-dwelling birds are chicken-like in both looks and habit. Most have stout bills, rounded wings, and heavy bodies. Primarily terrestrial, they are capable of short bursts of flight. Males are usually more brightly coloured than females. Diet consists of seeds, fruit, and buds.

## RUFFED GROUSE
*Bonasa umbellus*
43 cm (17 in.)

A mottled brown bird found in open woodlands throughout Alberta. Key field marks include a crested head and black-banded, fan-shaped tail. Males can sometimes be heard during breeding season as they drum their wings loudly in the air. Usually winters in coniferous forests. (Resident)

## SHARP-TAILED GROUSE
*Tympanuchus phasianellus*
46 cm (18 in.)

Fairly common in prairies and brushy, wooded areas. This large, brown bird is distinguished by its short, pointed tail and speckled breast. Tail shows white in flight. Each spring these birds flock to ancestral dancing grounds where males strut and fight for females. (Resident)

## GRAY PARTRIDGE
*Perdix perdix*
30 cm (12 in.)

This chunky, gray bird is found in brushy lowlands and grain-fields. Distinguished by its rusty face, barred flanks, and U-shaped belly patch. Note short tail. Introduced to Alberta from Hungary in 1908. (Resident)

## RING-NECKED PHEASANT
*Phasianus colchicus*
76 cm (30 in.)

Common in brushy margins of fields and forests in southern Alberta. Male is told by its shiny green head, red eye patch, white neck ring, and long tail. Female is mottled brown with a long tail. Introduced to the province in 1908. (Resident)

## PLOVERS

These wading birds are told from sandpipers by their thick necks, short bills and large eyes. Active feeders, they characteristically move about in short sprints. Sexes are similar.

## KILLDEER
*Charadrius vociferus*
25 cm (10 in.)

As its Latin name indicates, the Killdeer is a highly vocal bird. Common in fields and pastures, it is distinguished by its brown back, white breast, and two black neck bands. Rump shows orange in flight. Call is a shrill, repetitive *kill-dee, kill-dee* is repeated continuously. When their nest is approached, adults will often feign injury to lure intruders away from the area. (April-November)

## AVOCETS

This group of beautiful long-legged wading birds has slender bills and feeds on insects, seeds, and small aquatic animals. Sexes are similar.

### AMERICAN AVOCET
*Recurvirostra americana*
46 cm (18 in.)

Common in shallow ponds and marshes in southern Alberta. Told at a glance by its slender, upturned black bill and distinctive black and white plumage. Head and neck are tawny during the breeding season, and light gray the rest of the year. Feeds by working bill side to side while walking through the water. Call is a loud *wheek*.

## SANDPIPERS

Sandpipers are long-legged wading birds normally found along shorelines. Most are brownish and have slender bills which they use to probe the sand and mud for invertebrates. Species are largely differentiated by size, bill length and tail, rump and wing patterns. Sexes are similar in most species.

### LEAST SANDPIPER
*Calidris minutilla*
13 cm (5 in.)

This sparrow-sized sandpiper is a common migrant and abundant throughout the province in the spring and fall. Plummage is brown above and white belly below. Its yellow legs are a good field mark. Prefers grassy to open areas.

only during migration

## SPOTTED SANDPIPER
*Actitis macularia*
18 cm (7 in.)

Probably the best known sandpiper in the province, this solitary bird is found in a variety of habitats near water. It is distinguished in the summer by its darkly spotted light under-parts. Usually teeters back and forth on legs when walking. (April-September)

## COMMON SNIPE
*Gallinago gallinago*
28 cm (11 in.)

Found in marshes, bogs, and grassy sloughs. Similar to the Long-billed Dowitcher, the Common Snipe is generally browner and has more pro-nounced streaking on its head and back. When flushed, it flies off in an erratic, evasive manner. (April-October)

## LONG-BILLED DOWITCHER
*Limnodromus scolopaceus*
29 cm (11.5 in.)

A common migrant found flocking in wet meadows and along lakeshores. Told from most shorebirds by the length of its bill. Field marks include its rusty belly and dark breast bars. Feeds in shallow water and has a charac-teristic manner of repeatedly jabbing bill in and out of the mud like a sewing machine. Its similar cousin, the Short-billed Dowitcher, is also found in the province.

only during migration

### LESSER YELLOWLEGS
*Tringa flavipes* 25 cm (10 in.)
### GREATER YELLOWLEGS
*Tringa melanoleuca* 36 cm (14 in.)

Found near ponds, marshes, and bogs. Some of the first shore-birds to arrive each spring, these gray-brown birds are the only tall, long-legged sandpipers to have bright yellow legs. Note white rumps. They can be distinguished from each other by their size and call: the lesser has 1-3 note whistle; the greater has a 3-5 note whistle (April-September)

### WILLET
*Catoptrophorus semipalmatus*
39 cm (15.5 in.)

Found in wet meadows and along shorelines. At rest it can be told by its size, gray plum-age, dark legs, and thick bill. Key field mark is flashy black-and-white wing pattern dis-played in flight. Named for its call, a musical *pill-will-willet*.

### MARBLED GODWIT
*Limosa fedoa*
46 cm (18 in.)

Found on wet grasslands and the shores of marshes and ponds. A large shorebird, it is distinguished by its buff-brown plumage and long, slightly upturned (sometimes straight) bill. Wing linings are cinnamon. Its call is an accented *god-WIT, god-WIT*.

## LONG-BILLED CURLEW
*Numenius americanus*
58 cm (23 in.)

Found in open areas near water. Distinguished by its large size, buff-brown plumage, and long, downcurved bill. Shows bright cinnamon wing linings in flight. Call is a loud *cur-lew!, cur-lew!*

## PHALAROPES

A small group of long-necked, swimming sandpipers with distinctive lobed toes. In contrast to most bird species, the female is larger and more colourful than the male, and the male is responsible for building the nest, incubating the eggs, and raising the young. They feed on insects and small aquatic animals.

## WILSON'S PHALAROPE
*Phalaropus tricolor*
23 cm (9 in.)

Found near marshes, pools, and shallow lakes, this bird is identified by its needle-like bill, white rump, and dark, unstriped wings. In spring the female has a broad band on its face and neck, which blends from black to chestnut as it descends. The male is similar though duller. When feeding, the birds often spin about as they dab their bills in and out of the water.

## GULLS & TERNS

Gulls and terns are long-winged, web-footed birds typically found near water. Adults are usally gray and white: immature birds are brown. Sexes are similar. Species are distinguished from each other by wing patterns and bill colour. Gulls are larger then terns and have thick bills, square or rounded tails and long legs. They scavenge for food and will eat almost anything. Terns are smaller, more streamlined birds with pointed bills and forked tails. They feed by catching insects on the wing or by diving for fish from the air.

### FRANKLIN'S GULL
*Larus pipixcan*
38 cm (15 in.)

Commonly found near marshes and sloughs on the prairies. Adults are told by their black heads, orange beaks, and black-and-white tipped primaries. Breeds in large colonies. Unlike most gulls, it feeds primarily on insects. (April-September)

### RING-BILLED GULL
*Larus delawarensis*
48 cm (19 in.)

Found near lakes, rivers, fields, and dumps throughout eastern Alberta. Key field marks are its yellow eyes, yellow legs, and black-ringed, yellow bill. (March-November)

### CALIFORNIA GULL
*Larus californicus*
56 cm (22 in.)

Often found in the company of Ring-billed Gulls near lakes and rivers. One of the commoner gulls with black wing tips, it can be distinguished by its greenish legs. Lower bill is marked with red or red and black spots. (March-September)

## HERRING GULL
*Larus argentatus*
61 cm (24 in.)

Found near bodies of water and garbage dumps. Distinguished from similar gulls by its flesh-coloured legs. Varied diet includes carrion, garbage, eggs, young birds, and aquatic animals.

## BLACK TERN
*Chlidonias niger*
25 cm (10 in.)

Found in marshy habitats where insects are abundant. Black plumage and tern-like profile are diagnostic. Unlike most terns Black Terns frequently travel long distances from water in search of insects. (May-August)

## COMMON TERN
*Sterna hirundo*
38 cm (15 in.)

Found near open lakes and ponds. Identified in the field by its black cap, deeply forked tail, and red-orange, black-tipped bill. (April-October)

## DOVES

These familiar birds are common and widespread throughout the province. All species coo. They feed largely on seeds, grain, and insects.

### MOURNING DOVE
*Zenaida macroura*
30 cm (12 in.)

This common bird frequents prairies and grasslands where it feeds in open areas on grains and insects. More streamlined than the Rock Dove, it is distinguished by its tawny colour and long, pointed tail. Named for its mournful, cooing song. (April-October)

### ROCK DOVE
(Domestic Pigeon) *Columba livia*
36 cm (14 in.)

This introduced species is common in cities, towns, and farmlands. Typically blue-gray in colour, several variants also exist which range in colour from white to brown. Key field marks include white rump and black-banded tail. (Resident)

# OWLS

These square-shaped birds of prey have large heads, large eyes, and hooked bills. Large flattened areas around each eye form "facial disks" which help to amplify sound toward external ear flaps. Primarily nocturnal. Sexes are similar.

## GREAT HORNED OWL
*Bubo virginianus*
56 cm (22 in.)

Found in forests and woodlands. A large, dark brown bird, it is distinguished by its large size and prominent ear tufts. Plumage is heavily barred. Note yellow eyes and white throat. Feeds on small mammals and birds, and is sometimes spotted hunting during the day. The voice is a deep *hoo-hoo-hooooo*. It is Alberta's provincial bird.

## BURROWING OWL
*Athene cunicularia*
25 cm (10 in.)

A small owl found in open grassland and farmland in southern Alberta. Usually seen on or near the ground, it is recognized by its long legs, round head, and short tail. It often bobs up and down when restless or agitated. Commonly abroad during the day, it lives underground in abandoned rodent burrows.

## SHORT-EARED OWL
*Asio flammeus*
38 cm (15 in.)

This pigeon-sized owl is well known since it inhabits open country and is often active during the day. Told by bright yellow eyes bordered in black feathers. Ear tufts are barely perceptible. Often hovers over fields when hunting. Numbers often vary in accordance with rodent populations.

## HUMMINGBIRDS

The smallest birds, hummingbirds are named for the noise made by their wings as they beat rapidly during flight. All have long needle-like bills and extensible tongues which are used to extract nectar from flowers. Plumage is usually partially iridescent.

### RUBY-THROATED HUMMINGBIRD
*Archilochus colubris*
9 cm (3.5 in.)

This tiny bird is often found hovering in meadows and gardens near flowers. Plumage is green above, white below. Only the male has a bright red throat. Feeds primarily on nectar extracted from flowers. (May-September)

### RUFOUS HUMMINGBIRD
*Selasphorus rufus*
9 cm (3.5 in.)

Found in meadows and forests with abundant flowering plants. The male's red back is a key field mark. Female has a green back and red tail feathers.

## KINGFISHERS

This group of solitary, broad-billed birds are renowned for their fishing expertise. Acrobatic feeders, they habitually plunge into the water from great heights. Often found perched in trees bordering clear water.

### BELTED KINGFISHER
*Ceryle alcyon*
30 cm (12 in.)

This solitary bird is found near wooded ponds, lakes, and rivers throughout the province. It is told by its large size, ragged head crest, and long, broad bill. Often hovers over the water before diving after fish. Call is a loud rattle. (May-October)

## WOODPECKERS

These strong-billed birds are usually spotted perched along tree trunks where they chip away for insects beneath the bark. All have stiff tails which act like props as they forage along tree trunks. In spring, the males drum on dead limbs and other resonant objects (e.g., garbage cans, drainpipes) to establish their territories.

### DOWNY WOODPECKER
*Picoides pubescens*
15 cm (6 in.)

A small black-and-white woodpecker found in deciduous and mixed woods. Its key field mark is its long white back stripe. The male has a prominent red patch on back of head. Short, slender bill and small size help to distinguish it from the similar hairy woodpecker. (Resident)

## HAIRY WOODPECKER
*Picoides villosus*
23 cm (9 in.)

Commonly found in deciduous forests and river groves. It is similar to the Downy Woodpecker, but is larger in size and has a longer bill. The female is similar to male in both species but lacks red head patch. (Resident)

## YELLOW-BELLIED SAPSUCKER
*Sphyrapicus varius*
20 cm (8 in.)

Found in deciduous and mixed forests. A mottled black-and-white bird, it is identified by its red forehead and long white wing stripe. Male also has a red throat. Sapsuckers habitually drill orderly holes in the trunks of deciduous trees, and periodically return to feed on the sap and insects that collect there. (May-September)

## NORTHERN FLICKER
*Collaptes auratus*
30 cm (12 in.)

Found in open woodlands, these robin-sized birds are the commonest woodpeckers in the province. Key field marks include brown plumage, barred back, and black bib. Rump is white in flight. A newly designated species, it includes three formerly distinct species — the Yellow-shafted Flicker, Red-shafted Flicker, and Gilded Flicker — which have been found to interbreed freely. Only the former two occur in Alberta. Yellow-shafted males are distinguished by their yellow wing linings, black moustaches, and red head patches. Red-shafted males have red wing linings and red moustaches. Females of both species are similar to males but lack moustaches. (April-September)

# FLYCATCHERS

These compact birds characteristically sit on exposed perches and dart out to catch passing insects. Many species have bristles at the base of their bill. Sexes are similar.

### LEAST FLYCATCHER
*Empidonax minimus*
13 cm (5 in.)

 Common in wooded country and brushy areas. Identified as a tiny gray bird, white below, with white wing bars, a white eye ring, and bill bristles. Its call is a distinctive sharp *che-beK* and is repeated continuously. (May-August)

### WESTERN WOOD PEWEE
*Contopus sordidulus*
15 cm (6 in.)

 Common in deciduous and mixed woodlands. Similar to the Least Flycatcher, it is slightly larger, has a darker chest, and lacks an eye ring. Note the light wing bars. Usually inhabits the upper canopy of trees. Its call is a nasal *peeeer*. (May-August)

### EASTERN PHOEBE
*Sayornis phoebe*
18 cm (7 in.)

 Found near farms, towns, and open woodlands, the Eastern Phoebe often nests in the eaves of buildings and under bridges. An indistinct brown-gray bird, it habitually pumps its tail up and down when perching. Call is a clear *phoe-be*. (April-September)

### EASTERN KINGBIRD
*Tyrannus tyrannus*
20 cm (8 in.)

This aggressive, noisy bird is found in open woodlands and shrubby meadows. Distinguished by its dark back, black mask, white underparts, and the white band on the tip of its tail. Highly territorial, it will actively defend its nesting areas against intruders, including man. (May-August)

## LARKS

Larks are highly terrestrial birds with musical voices. Typically streaked brown. They have elongated back claws on their feet. A single member of this Old World family is found in Alberta.

### HORNED LARK
*Eremophila alpestris*
18 cm (7 in.)

Abundant on the prairies, this highly terrestrial bird ranges over fields and shorelines. Brown in colour, it is distinguished by its yellow face, black breast mark, and black "horns." Nests and feeds on the ground. One of our earliest spring migrants, it often lays its eggs before the snow has completely melted. (February-November; some overwinter)

## SWALLOWS

These streamlined, acrobatic fliers have short legs, short bills, long pointed wings, and long tails (often forked). Their wide mouths are adapted for scooping up insects on the wing. Often seen perched in groups along power lines and fences. Flight is undulating and graceful.

### BANK SWALLOW
*Riparia riparia*
13 cm (5 in.)

Bank swallows are often found near marshes, streams, and rivers in large colonies. Distinguished by a brown back, white underparts, and dark neckband. It is named for its habit of nesting in holes in the sides of steep banks. Its song is a dry trill of *trrii, trrii, trrii*. (May-August)

### CLIFF SWALLOW
*Hirundo pyrrhonota*
15 cm (6 in.)

Common throughout the province. Field marks include white forehead, orange rump, and square tail. Often found near bridges and buildings, which are preferred nesting sites. Look for distinctive jug-like nests constructed from mud pellets. Song is a pleasant series of grating and creaking *cherrs*. (May-August)

## TREE SWALLOW
*Tachycineta bicolor*
15 cm (6 in.)

Found throughout woodlands and open prairies, usually near water. Identified by its blue-green back and white breast. Often glides in circles when airborne. Song is a variable, three-note, burbling twitter. (April-August)

## BARN SWALLOW
*Hirundo rustica*
18 cm (7 in.)

This is a familiar swallow, found near farms and other rural habitations. It can be identified by its dark blue back, light underparts, and rusty throat and forehead. Note its deeply forked tail. Often nests in building rafters. Its song is a cheery twittering. (May-September)

## PURPLE MARTIN
*Progne subis*
20 cm (8 in.)

This large swallow is commonly found in open, wooded areas in cities and towns in central Alberta. Distinguished by its large size, purple-black back, and dark breast (black in male; gray in female), it frequently glides in circles when flying. The purple martin nests in colonies, and is easily attracted to multi-celled bird houses. (May-August)

## CROWS & ALLIES

These large, omnivorous birds are familiar to most people. Most have stout bills with bristles near the base. Sexes are similar.

### GRAY JAY
*Perisoreus canadensis*
28 cm (11 in.)

Also known as the Canada Jay and Whiskey Jack, this bird inhabits coniferous forests. Distinguished by its fluffy gray plumage, white face, and dark neck patch, it is one of the tamest birds in the province, and will often approach campers for food scraps. Feeds largely on conifer seeds. (Resident)

### BLUE JAY
*Cyanocitta cristata*
30 cm (12 in.)

Commonly found in woodlands and open areas, the blue jay often inhabits cities and towns during winter when food is scarce. Told by its crested head, blue back, and black neckband. Easily attracted to feeders. (Resident)

### AMERICAN CROW
*Corvus brachyrhynchos*
48 cm (19 in.)

Very common in a variety of habitats throughout the province. A familiar sight in rural areas, it is identified by its black plumage and black bill. A dedicated omnivore, it eats everything from insects and grain, to small birds and refuse. Call is a distinct *caw*. (March-October; a few overwinter)

## COMMON RAVEN
*Corvus corax*
64 cm (25 in.)

Common in wilderness and open country throughout the foothills and northern reaches of the province. Similar to the crow, it is distinguished by its larger size, heavier beak, keeled tail, and low, croaking call. Primarily a scavenger, it is often found near dumps and refuse sites. (Resident)

## BLACK-BILLED MAGPIE
*Pica pica*
76 cm (30 in.)

Found near fields, pastures, thickets, and roadsides throughout the province. Distinguished by its black hood, long, wedge-shaped tail, and white wing patches. Often seen scavenging in fields and along roadsides. Feeds primarily on small mammals and insects.(March-October; many overwinter)

# CHICKADEES

These small, plump birds have lareage heads, small, straight bills and fluffy plumage. They are very active and inquisitive. Diet consists of seeds, berries and insects.

## BLACK-CAPPED CHICKADEE
*Parus atricapillus*
13 cm (5 in.)

Common in forests and semi-wooded areas. Identified by its small size, fluffy gray plumage, black cap and chin, and white face patch. Abundant in cities and towns during winter, it is easily attracted to feeders. Its call is a clear *chick-a-dee-dee-dee*. (Resident)

## BOREAL CHICKADEE
*Parus hudsonicus*
13 cm (5 in.)

Found primarily in dense coniferous forests. It can be distinguished by its brown head and back, rusty sides, and white cheeks; the sexes are similar. Call is a blurry, slow *chick-a-day-day*. (Resident)

## NUTHATCHES

Nuthatches are stout little birds with thin, sharp bills and stumpy tails. They have strong legs and feet and are typically spotted clambering about on the tree trunks and branches in all directions (even upside-down). Diet consists of insects, seeds, nuts and fruit.

### RED-BREASTED NUTHATCH
*Sitta canadensis*
13 cm (5 in.)

Found in coniferous and mixed wood forests. This chunky little bird creeps about on tree trunks and branches searching for insects beneath the bark. Habitually descends trunks head first. Key field marks are black-and-white eye stripes, and short tail. Its call is a nasal *hee-hee-hee-hee*. (April-September)

## WRENS

These plump little brown birds often carry their tail cocked over their back. Wings are short and rounded. They spend much of their time on the ground foraging for insects.

### HOUSE WREN
*Troglodytes aedon*
13 cm (5 in.)

Found in thickets and wooded areas near farmlands and towns. An indistinct brown bird, it has the unusual habit of cocking its short tail over its back. This aggressive little bird moves about in quick, jerky motions, often scolding intruders. Song is a gurgling melody. (May-September)

## THRUSHES & ALLIES

This family of woodland birds includes the kinglets, thrushes and bluebirds. Kinglets are tiny birds known for their crowns and busy habits. Thrushes and bluebirds are larger slender-billed, wide-eyed birds, many of which are good singers.

### MOUNTAIN BLUEBIRD
*Sialia currucoides*
18 cm (7 in.)

Found in semi-open woodlands in central and southern Alberta. Male's turquoise plumage is unmistakable. Tawny female shows turquoise on wings, especially in flight. Feeds largely on insects. Population has been threatened in recent years owing to the abundance of aggressive starlings and house sparrows. An active nest box program has helped to re-establish this species in Alberta. (April-October)

### SWAINSON'S THRUSH
*Catharus ustulatus*
18 cm (7 in.)

Found in the under-growth of conifer-ous and mixed forests. Brown with a speckled breast, it is distinguished by its eye ring and buffy cheeks.(May-October)

### AMERICAN ROBIN
*Turdus migratorius*
25 cm (10 in.)

Very common in towns, fields, and open woodlands. A familiar bird to most, it is told by its gray back and rusty breast. Usually forages on the ground for insects, snails, and worms. (April-October; a few overwinter in southern Alberta)

### RUBY-CROWNED KINGLET
*Regulus calendula*
10 cm (4 in.)

Found in mixed and coniferous forests. A tiny, green bird, it is distinguished by its short tail, broken eye ring, and two white wing patches. Habitually flicks wings nervously while perching. The male's red cap is often difficult to spot. Its song is comprised of three to four notes in variable combinations, e.g., *see, see, see, too, too, too, tee-do-da-dee* . (May-September)

## WAXWINGS

This group of gregarious birds are named for their red wing marks which look like waxy droplets. Told at a glance by their sleek, crested heads and yellow-tipped tails.

### CEDAR WAXWING
*Bombycilla cedrorum*
18 cm (7 in.)

Commonly found in open deciduous woods. Identified by its crested head, yellow abdomen, and yellow-tipped tail. Undertail coverts (where tail connects with body) are white. Diet consists largely of berries and insects. (June-September)

### BOHEMIAN WAXWING
*Bombycilla garrulus*
20 cm (8 in.)

Found in coniferous and mixed forests during the summer. Distinguished from the Cedar Waxwing by its grey belly, white wing patches, and rusty undertail coverts . Large flocks often travel into suburban areas during winter to feast on the berries of ornamental trees and shrubs. (Resident)

## SHRIKES

Noted for their aggressive behaviour, they are told by their gray plumage, black masks, and stout, hooked bills. Nicknamed "butcher birds", Shrikes often impale prey on thorns or barbed wire. Feed largely on small mammals, birds, and insects.

### LOGGERHEAD SHRIKE
*Lanius ludovicianus*
23 cm (9 in.)

Found in open farming country with scattered trees. Gray in colour, it is distinguished by its black eye patches, hooked bill, and black wings. Wings show white patches in flight. Often perches on wires or exposed branches. Flight is undulating. (April-August)

## STARLINGS

A single member of this varied Old World family of birds occurs in Alberta.

### EUROPEAN STARLING
*Sturnus vulgaris*
23 cm (9 in.)

This introduced species is found in a variety of habitats throughout the province. Similar to a blackbird, it is distinguished by its chubby profile and short tail. Bill has yellow hue at certain times of the year. It usually travels in huge flocks. Considered a pest by many, the starling is an aggressive bird that competes with native species for food and choice nesting sights. Some feel that the decline of the Mountain Bluebird population is directly linked to the success of this bird. (March-October; some may overwinter)

# VIREOS

Vireos are small birds with hooked bills which are more often heard then seen. Plumage usually is olive-gray above, light below, with yellow sides. They build fragile cup-like nests suspended between forked twigs.

### RED-EYED VIREO
*Vireo olivaceus*
15 cm (6 in.)

A small, green bird found in deciduous and mixed forests. Distinguished by its gray cap and black-banded, white eye stripes it inhabits rural and urban areas. Its red eyes are a poor field mark. Its song is a monotonous repetition of small phrases which rise and fall. (May-September)

## WOOD WARBLERS & ALLIES

Members of this large family of highly active, insect-eating birds are distinguished from other small birds by their thin, pointed bills. Most species display some yellow or green. Males tend to be more brightly coloured than females and are the only singers. The best field marks for warblers are head markings and wing bars.

### TENNESSEE WARBLER
*Vermivora peregrina*
13 cm (5 in.)

Commonly found in deciduous and mixed forests. Field marks include gray head, white breast, light eyebrows, and black line through eye. Head and breast fade to yellow in the fall. Three-parted song is a loud *tene-tene-tene-tene-zip-zip-see-see-see*. (May-September)

## YELLOW WARBLER
*Dendroica petechia*
13 cm (5 in.)

Common near shrubs and thickets in river valleys, coulees, and urban areas. This bright yellow warbler, is distinguished from similar species by its yellow-spotted tail. Males also have rusty streaks on their breast. Song is a cheery *sweet,sweet,sweet*. (May- September)

## BLACKPOLL WARBLER
*Dendroica striata*
15 cm (6 in.)

A solitary bird found primarily in coniferous forests. The streaked, gray male is told by its black cap, white cheeks, and light double wing bars. Females are duller and lack a black cap. Song is a repetitive *zee-zee-zee-zee-zee*. (May-September)

## YELLOW-RUMPED WARBLER
*Dendroica coronata*
15 cm (6 in.)

Commonly found in coniferous forests. Bluish male is identified by its black breast, yellow cap and yellow rump. A newly designated species, it includes two formerly distinct species — the Myrtle Warbler (top) and Audubon's Warbler (bottom)— which have since been found to interbreed freely. The Myrtle male has a white throat. The Audubon male is told by its yellow throat and thick white wing patch. Brown females have markings similar to the males on their throats and rumps. (April-September)

## AMERICAN REDSTART
*Setophaga ruticilla*
15 cm (6 in.)

An active insectivorous bird common in deciduous and mixed woods. Distinctive black male has bright orange wing and tail patches. Females are olive coloured with yellowish wing and tail patches. Song is a clear *zee-zee-zee-zee-zee-ZEE*, or *teetza-teetza-teetza-teetza*. (May-September)

## OVENBIRD
*Seiurus aurocapillus*
15 cm (6 in.)

Found in deciduous and mixed woods, it commonly forages on the forest floor for insects. An olive-coloured bird, it is distinguished by its pink legs and black-bordered, orange crown. Easily identified by its song— a loud *teach-er, teach-er*. Named for its domed nest which is shaped like a dutch oven. (May-September)

## BLACKBIRDS & ALLIES

A diverse group of birds, ranging from iridescent black birds to the bright orange and yellow of tanagers and orioles. The different species inhabit a wide variety of habitats, but all have conical, sharp-pointed bills.

### BROWN-HEADED COWBIRD
*Molothrus ater*
18 cm (7 in.)

Common on farmlands and fields, they are often spotted feeding near domestic livestock. Male is distinguished by its brown head and finch-like bill. Gray female is noted for her parasitic habit of laying eggs in the nest of other birds. While some species remove the new egg, most will raise the orphaned cowbird as their own. (May-August)

### BREWER'S BLACKBIRD
*Euphagus cyanocephalus*
23 cm (9 in.)

Common in fields and pastures in the prairie and parkland regions. Key field marks are iridescent purple head and green-black body. Often perches in large groups along fences and wires. Forages on the ground for grain and insects. (April-November)

## RED-WINGED BLACKBIRD
*Agelaius phoeniceus*
25 cm (10 in.)

Found in sloughs, marshes, and wet fields, the Red-winged Blackbird usually nests in reeds or tall grass near water. The black male has distinctive red shoulder patches. The brown female is heavily streaked and lacks shoulder patches. Normally found in large flocks. (April-October) The less common Yellow-headed Blackbird *(Xanthocephalus xanthocephalus)* is found in similar habitats.

## COMMON GRACKLE
*Quiscalus quiscula*
30 cm (12 in.)

A large blackbird found near farms and towns in moist fields and woodlands. Identified by its glossy blue-black plumage and long, keel-shaped tail. Feeds along the ground on insects, small animals and refuse. (April-September)

## WESTERN MEADOWLARK
*Sturnella neglecta*
18 cm (7 in.)

Common in grassy fields, meadows, and marshes. Key field marks are long bill, bright yellow breast, white-edged tail, and dark V-shaped neckband. Flute-like, gurgling song is also distinctive. (March-October)

## NORTHERN ORIOLE
*Icterus galbula*
20 cm (8 in.)

Found primarily in open deciduous forests. A newly designated species, it includes two formerly distinct species — the Baltimore Oriole (top) and Bullock's Oriole (bottom) — which have been found to interbreed freely where their ranges overlap. The male of the Baltimore subspecies has a black head and bright orange breast and rump. The olive female has yellow-orange breast. The Bullock's male is similar but has an orange face, black eye line, and a large white wing patch. Olive female has a yellow breast and a white belly. Both subspecies build distinctive pouch-like nests. (May-August)

## SPARROWS

Sparrows are mostly brown birds with short thick, seed-cracking bills. Largely distinguished by tail, face and wing patterns.

## CLAY-COLOURED SPARROW
*Spizella pallida*
13 cm (5 in.)

Found in brushy areas throughout the prairies and parklands. Key field marks are the streaked crown, brown cheeks, light eye stripe, and unstreaked breast. Song is a series of low buzzes. (April-September)

## CHIPPING SPARROW
*Spizella passerina*
13 cm (5 in.)

Inhabiting primarily open forests, this sparrow is distinguished by its red cap, white eyebrow line, black line through eye, and unstreaked breast. Song is a repetitive, sharp *chip*. (May-September)

## SAVANNAH SPARROW
*Passerculus sandwichensis*
14 cm (5.5 in.)

Commonly found feeding along the ground near sloughs and marshes in fields and grasslands. A brown, streaked bird, it is distinguished by its dull yellow eyebrows and short, notched tail. When approached, it often flies away for a short distance before landing. (May-September)

## VESPER SPARROW
*Pooecetes gramineus*
15 cm (6 in.)

Common in meadows, grasslands, and grain fields, it is one of the best known sparrows in the province. Key field marks are its light eye ring and white-edged tail. Nests on the ground. Song consists of two low notes followed by two higher notes. (May-September)

## SONG SPARROW
*Me
lospiza melodia*
15 cm (6 in.)

Common in bushes and woodlands near water. Similar to the
Savannah Sparrow, it is distinguished by its long tail and dark
breast spot. Often pumps its tail
in flight. Melodious song
usually begins with three to four similar
notes. (April-September)

## WHITE-THROATED SPARROW
*Zonotrichia albicollis*
18 cm (7 in.)

Found in brushy areas in coniferous and mixed forests. Is distinguished from other sparrows by
its white throat, black and white
striped crown, and yellow facial
mark (not always evident).
Varying song consists of clear whistle-like
notes, in a melody similar to *O-CAN-ada*.
(May-October)

# FINCHES

Members of this family are highly coloured and have short, thick, seed-cracking
bills. Diet consists of seeds, berries, buds and insects.

## AMERICAN GOLDFINCH
*Carduelis tristis*
13 cm (5 in.)

One of the last birds to arrive in
the late spring, they are often
found in wooded groves and
bushy areas. Male is bright yellow
with a black cap, tail, and wings
and a white rump. Olive-coloured
female is similarly marked, but lacks a cap.
Often found in flocks. Can be identified on
the wing by its deeply undulating flight.
Canary-like song is bright and cheery.
(June-September)

### PINE SISKIN
*Carduelis pinus*
13 cm (5 in.)

Common in coniferous and mixed forests, these birds are easily attracted to feeders. Told by their heavily streaked plumage and notched tail. Small yellow patches on wings and tail are most prominent in flight. Often found flocking in the tops of trees. (May-September)

### COMMON REDPOLL
*Carduelis flammea*
13 cm (5 in.)

Found in birch stands and grassy fields, this common winter visitor arrives when most birds are leaving the province. Key field marks are the red cap and black beard. Males also have a pink breast. Often found foraging on the ground for seeds. (October-April)

### RED CROSSBILL
*Loxia curvirostra*
15 cm (6 in.)

Found in coniferous forests in the mountain region. Told by its red body, dark wings and dark tail. Bill is crossed near the tip, though this is often hard to discern in the field. Feeds primarily on conifer seeds. Numbers often vary in relation to the abundance of cones. (Resident).

## DARK-EYED JUNCO
*Junco hyemalis*
15 cm (6 in.)

Found in brushy fields and meadows bordering coniferous and mixed forests. Key field marks are dark head, white bill, and white belly, and white-edged tail. A newly designated species, it includes four formerly distinct species — the Slate-coloured Junco (top), Oregon Junco (bottom), Gray-headed Junco, and White-winged Junco — which have been observed to interbreed freely where their ranges overlap. Of these, only the first two occur in Alberta. The slate-coloured version has gray sides and a gray back. The Oregon version has a black head and a brown back. (April-September)

## WEAVER FINCHES

A single member of this Old World family occurs in Alberta.

## HOUSE SPARROW
*Passer domesticus*
15 cm (6 in.)

Very common throughout the province in a variety of habitats. Black throat and brown nape of male are diagnostic. Females and young are dull brown with a light eye stripe. Common in flocks. This species and the starling are responsible for the near extinction of Mountain Bluebirds and other native cavity nesting birds. (Resident)

# ALBERTA AMPHIBIANS

Amphibians are smooth-skinned, cold-blooded animals which live in moist habitats. They are able to breathe through lungs, skin, gills, or a combination of all three. The two distinct groups of amphibians found in Alberta are: salamanders, and frogs and toads.

Like fish, amphibians are unable to maintain a constant body temperature. Their activity levels are largely determined by their environment, being enhanced in warm weather and reduced in cold.

While amphibians live much of their lives on land, they still depend on a watery environment to complete their life cycle. Most reproduce by laying eggs in or near the water. The young hatch as swimming larvae, or tadpoles, which breathe by means of gills. After a short developmental period, the larvae metamorphose into young adults with lungs and legs.

## HOW TO IDENTIFY AMPHIBIANS

Of the amphibians, the frogs and toads are probably the easiest to observe since they loudly announce their presence to all within earshot during breeding season. Salamanders are far more secretive and rarely venture out of their cool, moist habitats.

The best time to look for frogs and toads is just after dark when they are most vocal. If you approach the water quietly with an artificial light, you should be able to get close enough to identify the different species.

# SALAMANDERS

Salamanders are tailed, lizard-like creatures which inhabit moist areas either on or under the ground. Unlike lizards, they have a smooth skin and lack claws and ear openings. Seldom seen, they live in dark, moist habitats and are typically nocturnal and secretive. They are most active in the spring during the breeding season and in fall. Fertilization is internal but is not accomplished by copulation. During the mating activity of most salamanders, the male releases a small packet of sperm. The female brushes against the packet, and draws it into her body. The sperm are kept in the female's body until she ovulates, which may be months later. Most species lay their eggs in water. Both adults and larvae are carnivorous and feed on invertebrates, worms, and insects. Some salamanders have the unique ability to regenerate limbs or tails lost to predators.

## TIGER SALAMANDER
*Ambystoma tigrinum* var. *melanostictum*
to 25 cm (10 in.)

A stout, large-headed salamander found in ponds, marshes, and moist woods in the prairie and parkland regions. Black, shiny skin is irregularly blotched with light-coloured spots. One of the mole salamanders, it spends most of its time underground in burrows. Best seen at night or after rains during spring breeding season. Diet consists of worms, insects, amphibians, and small animals.

## TOADS

Both toads and frogs are squat, tail-less amphibians common near ponds and lakes throughout the province. All have large heads, large eyes, long hind legs, and long, sticky tongues which they use to catch insects. Most have well-developed ears and a strong voice. Only males are vocal, and their breeding choruses can be deafening. Toads can be distinguished from frogs by their dry warty skin, and prominent glands (parotoid) behind their eyes. May also have prominent swellings between their eyes (bosses). When handled roughly by would-be predators, the warts and glands secret a substance which makes the toads extremely unpalatable. Contrary to popular belief, handling toads does not cause warts.

### CANADA TOAD
*Bufo hemiophrys*
to 10 cm (4 in.)

Abundant in marshes, ponds, and ditches throughout much of the province. Distinguished by its brown to green colour, light dorsal stripe, and prominent boss. Often buries itself at night beneath loose soil or leaves. Diurnal.

### BOREAL TOAD
*Bufo boreas*
to 12 cm (4.7 in.)

Found in or near water in the foothills or mountains. Dusky in colour, it can be recognized by its white dorsal stripe and the lack of a boss between its eyes. Warts contrast with body colour and are often tinged with rust. Active during twilight, it often lives in rodent burrows.

# FROGS

Unlike toads, frogs have smooth skin, slim waists, prominent dorsal ridges, and lack parotid glands. Like toads, males initiate mating by calling for females. When he finds a mate, he clasps her in water and fertilizes the eggs as they are laid. The eggs initially hatch into fish-like tadpoles which breathe through gills and feed on vegetation. They later transform into young adults by developing limbs and lungs, and absorbing their tails. They feed primarily on insects and crustaceans.

## WOOD FROG
*Rana sylvatica*
to 6 cm (2.4 in.)

Common in damp woods and wet grasslands, it often ranges far from water after breeding in early spring. Varies in colour from brown to pink. It can be recognized by its dark eye patches, white belly, and white jaw stripe. Call is a series of short, duck-like quacks. Diurnal. Hibernates in forest litter during winter.

## BOREAL CHORUS FROG
*Pseudacris triseriata*
to 4 cm (1.6 in.)

Common in grassy and wooded areas near shallow water. A member of the tree frog family, it is not a true frog. Typically olive-skinned, it can be recognized by the thick, dark stripes on its face and back. Note white upper lip and pointed snout. Vocal primarily during breeding season (April-June), its chirping call can be mimicked by dragging a fingernail over a comb. Nocturnal.

# ALBERTA REPTILES

Reptiles are fully terrestrial, cold-blooded vertebrates which have scaly skin. The group is represented in Alberta by turtles, lizards and snakes.

## HOW TO IDENTIFY REPTILES

The Western Painted Turtle, our only native species, often basks on rocks and logs near water. They are wary and should be approached cautiously. The Horned Lizard is a master of disguise and often lies very still in sandy areas in the vicinity of anthills.

The best time to look for snakes is in the early morning or late afternoon when it's not too hot. Look in meadows, fields, woods, or on the margins of ponds, checking under sun-warmed logs and rocks where they may be resting. The bullsnake and rattlesnake often sun themselves in open areas.

Since there are so few species of reptiles in the province, field identification for all but the garter snakes (whose stripe colours may vary) is simple. Be careful when handling garter snakes as they will often bite when provoked.

# TURTLES

Turtles are easily distinguished by their large bony shells. The shell is formed from widened ribs and serves to protect the turtle from most predators. Like all reptiles, turtles are air breathers and possess lungs. They are most active in spring during mating season. Females lay their eggs in holes excavated in soft soil near water. The young hatch either in late summer or the following spring, and are independent from birth. Most are omnivores and eat a wide variety of plant and animal matter.

### PAINTED TURTLE
*Chrysemys picta* var. *belli*
to 25 cm (10 in.)

Found in the Milk River drainage (see p.95), this is the only turtle native to Alberta. Distinguished by its smooth, green shell marked by an irregular pattern of yellow lines. Often spotted basking in the sun on partially submerged rocks or logs. Feeds on vegetation, crustaceans, and insects.

# LIZARDS

Lizards are scaly skinned reptiles which typically have moveable eyelids, visible ear openings, claws, and toothod jaws. Most lay eggs, though in some species the females retain the eggs in their bodies and give birth to live young. Highly terrestrial, lizards are well adapted for travel on land and have a more upright stance than amphibians. They have yet to penetrate far into Canada as they are fond of hot climates .

### SHORT-HORNED LIZARD
*Phrynosoma douglasii*
to 8 cm (3 in.)

Found on sandy soil in coulees in the extreme southeastern Alberta. Although it is relatively rare, this species has been included here since it is our only native lizard. A gray-brown, toad-sized creature it is distin-guished by the rows of sharp spines pro-jecting from its back and sides. It eats mostly insects, and can be spotted basking in the vicinity of anthills. Active during the day.

## SNAKES

Snakes are limbless reptiles with dry, scaly skin, toothed jaws, no ear openings or eyelids, and a single row of belly scales. They move by contracting their muscles in waves and undulating over the ground. All are carnivorous and swallow their prey whole. They flick their tongues in and out constantly to taste and smell the air around them. Most continue to grow in length during their life and shed their outer skin periodically. Only one Alberta species — the Prairie Rattlesnake — is considered dangerous.

### RED-SIDED GARTER SNAKE
*Thamnophis sirtalis* var. *parietalis*
to 1.2 m (47 in.)

This dark snake is commonly found near water in meadows, farmlands, and valleys. Distinguished in the field by the red or orange bars between its yellow dorsal stripe and yellow side stripes. A good swimmer it is the most common snake in North America.

### PLAINS GARTER SNAKE
*Thamnophis radix* var. *haydeni*
to 1.7 m (67 in.)

Found near ponds, and streams and marshes in the grassland and parkland regions. Brown-green in colour, it is distinguished by its prominent orange back stripe and yellow side stripes. Note double row of squarish black spots between stripes. Eats frogs, fish, small mammals, and insects.

### WANDERING GARTER SNAKE
*Thamnophis elegans* var. *vagrans*
to 1.7 m (67 in.)

Found in both terrestrial and aquatic habitats in southern Alberta. Yellow-orange dorsal stripe extends length of body. Identified by its checkerboard pattern of dark marks between its back and side stripes. Often enters the water to feed or escape predation. May be seen basking in the open early in the day.

## BULLSNAKE
*Pituophis melanoleucus* var. *sayi*
to 2.5 m (98 in).

Found on farmland and prairies in southern Alberta. Distinguished by its large size, yellow colour, and the dark blotches on its back and sides. Though non-poisonous, it imitates a rattlesnake when threatened by coiling up, hissing loudly, vibrating its tail, and striking out at its aggressor. Eats primarily small rodents and is valued for pest control on farms. It is also capable of climbing trees to raid bird nests.

## PRAIRIE RATTLESNAKE
*Crotalus viridis* var. *viridis*
to 1.3 m (51 in.)

Found in river valleys and dry prairies in southeastern Alberta. A darkly blotched, green-brown snake, it is best identified by its tail rattle which it vibrates when threatened. Note flattened head and defined neck. A pit viper, it has heat sensing areas between its eye and nostril which help it to detect prey. Enlarged front fangs have hollow canals which inject poison into prey when it strikes. Eats mostly rodents. Large numbers often hibernate in common dens. The least poisonous of rattlesnakes, its bite is seldom fatal to man.

# ALBERTA FISH

Fish are cold-blooded vertebrates which live in the water, have streamlined bodies covered in scales, possess fins, and breath by means of gills. Alberta is home to 49 species which are all members of the class of bony fishes known as Osteichthyes.

Fish are characterized by their size, shape, feeding habits, and habitat preferences. Given their cold-blooded nature, water temperature greatly controls their activity and rate of body functions. All have senses of taste, sight, touch, smell and hearing, though they lack external ears. They have small brains and a two-chambered heart. The pumping action of the heart is enhanced by muscular contractions which occur as the fish swims.

Fish swim by flexing their body from side to side. The dorsal and anal fins act as keels, and the paired fins help steer the fish, and can also act as brakes. Many also possess an internal air bladder which acts as a depth regulator. By secreting gases into the bladder or absorbing gases from it, they vary the depth at which they swim.

Most fish reproduce by laying eggs freely in the water. As the female lays the eggs, the male fertilizes them by discharging milt over them. Eggs of different species may float, sink, become attached to vegetation or be buried. Survival rates are often influenced by environmental factors.

Of the 23 species of fish in the book, 13 occur in all three major river drainage basins.

## HOW TO IDENTIFY FISHES

First, note the size, shape and colour of the fish. Are there any distinguishing field marks like the double dorsal fins of the perches or downturned lips of the suckers? Is the body thin or torpedo-shaped? Note the orientation and placement of the fins on the body. Consult the text for key field marks and identifying characteristics.

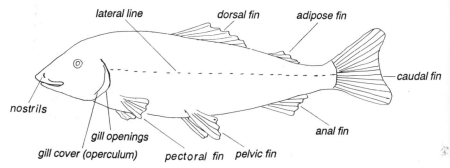

Great Slave Lake

SLAVE

*Bistcho Lake*

HAY

*Hay River*

High Level

*River*

Fort Chipewyan

*Lake Claire*

*Slave River*

*Lake Athabasca*

LAKE CLAIRE

PEACE

*Peace*

*Birch River*

*River*

Fort McMurray

Peace River

Grande Prairie

*Smoky River*

*Lesser Slave Lake*

ATHABASCA

Athabasca

*Athabasca*

BEAVER

Whitecourt

*North Saskatchewan R.*

St. Paul

Edmonton

Lloydminster

NORTH SASKATCHEWAN

Jasper

Wetaskiwin

BATTLE

Rocky Mountain House

Stettler

Provost

Red Deer

SOUNDING

RED    DEER

Drumheller

*Red*

Oyen

Banff

*Deer    River*

Calgary

BOW

*Bow River*

Brooks

*South Saskatchewan*

OLDMAN

*Oldman    River*

Medicine Hat

Lethbridge

SOUTH SASKATCHEWAN

MILK

## Drainage Basins

Continental Basins

- Arctic Ocean
- Hudson Bay
- Gulf of Mexico

Major Sub-basins

ATHABASCA

100 kilometres

## GOLDEYE & ALLIES

This ancient family of large-eyed, wide-bodied fish has two surviving members, one of which is found in Alberta. They possess toothed jaws, but lack an adipose fin.

### GOLDEYE
*Hiodon alosoides*
to 46 cm (18 in.)

Found in large silty rivers, shallow lakes, and ponds. A wide, flattened fish, it is told by its silvery sides, white belly, and yellow eyes. Its dorsal fin originates behind the middle of the body. Feeds on insects, invertebrates, small fish and aquatic animals.

## WHITEFISH

These fork-tailed, small-headed fish are found throughout America, Europe and Asia. All have fleshy adipose fins, big, loosely attached scales and few or no teeth.

### CISCO
*Coregonus artedii*
to 30 cm (12 in.)

A silvery-blue fish found in deep lakes and streams. Similar to the Lake Whitefish, it is distinguished by its long lower jaw which extends beyond the upper jaw. Snout is pointed. Feeds on plankton and invertebrates.

### LAKE WHITEFISH
*Coregonus clupeaformis*
to 60 cm (24 in.)

Common in lakes throughout Alberta, it is told by its silvery sides and rounded snout. Back is often humped, and lower jaw does not extend beyond margin of upper jaw. Dorsal colour ranges from olive green to blue. The most important commercial fish in the province, it feeds on insects, snails, and plankton.

## MOUNTAIN WHITEFISH
*Prosopium williamsoni*
to 45 cm (18 in.)

Abundant in streams and shallow lakes. Distinguished by its gray-brown head and back and silvery sides. Sometimes confused with Arctic Grayling, it has a much smaller dorsal fin. Largely a bottom feeder, it rises for surface insects on occasion.

## TROUT

Trout have elongated bodies, small scales, large mouth with numerous teeth and are fond of cool water. Almost all have an adipose fin. Diet consists of fish, insects and plankton.

### BROWN TROUT
*Salmo trutta*
to 60 cm (24 in.)

This introduced European species is found in streams and lakes in southwestern Alberta. Light brown in colour, it is the only trout with red and black body spots. Some side spots may have light-coloured outlines. An intelligent, cautious fish, it is generally considered to be the hardest sport fish to land in the province. Feeds on insects, fish, and crustaceans.

### CUTTHROAT TROUT
*Salmo clarki* var. *lewisi*
to 61 cm (24 in.)

Found in cold streams and lakes in southwestern Alberta. Distinctive red streak along inner edge of the lower jaw is good field mark. Throat and belly of spawners may also be red. Upper half of body is usually dark-spotted. Feeds largely on small fish.

## RAINBOW TROUT
*Salmo gairdneri*
to 60 cm (24 in.)

Heavily stocked throughout southwestern Alberta, it is abundant in streams, reservoirs, and lakes. This silvery fish is named for the distinctive rainbow band running down its side (most prominent during spawning season - April to July). Dark spots occur along back, upper fins, and tail. The sea-run variety of this species is referred to as Steelhead.

## BROOK TROUT
*Salvelinus fontinalis*
to 56 cm (22 in.)

This colourful fish is found in streams, ponds and shallow lakes in the mountain region. Green-purple in colour, it is distinguished by its numerous red spots with blue haloes and its dark-spotted dorsal fin. Note white stripes on leading edges of lower fins. Feeds on a wide variety of invertebrates, fish and insects.

## BULL TROUT
*Salvelinus confluentus*
to 65 cm (26 in.)

A native fish, it is found in cold lakes and streams. Gray-green back and silvery sides are covered with red, orange and yellow spots. Note large jaws and gently forked tail. Feeds on small fish, larvae and invertebrates.

## LAKE TROUT
*Salvelinus namaycush*
to 1.2 m (48 in.)

Found primarily in deep, cold lakes. Green-brown body is covered with numerous gray spots which extend onto the dorsal and tail fin. Tail is deeply forked. Diet consists of fish, crustaceans, and insects.

## ARCTIC GRAYLING
*Thymallus arcticus*
to 60 cm (24 in.)

Found in cold, clear streams and lakes. Purple-gray body is flecked with dark spots. Easily distinguished by its large, mauve-spotted dorsal fin. An aggressive fighter when hooked, it is a favourite of anglers. Feeds primarily on insects.

## PIKE

Pike are distinguished at a glance by their long, narrow bodies and flattened, duck-like snouts. The dorsal and anal fins are set well back on the body, and the adipose fin is absent. They all live in shallow, reedy waters along clear lakes and ponds. Pikes will eat almost anything including: fish, amphibians, ducklings and muskrats.

## NORTHERN PIKE
*Esox lucius*
to 1.2 m (48 in.)

Very common along the weedy margins of lakes, ponds and streams. Torpedo-shaped, green body is covered with pale oval and bar-shaped spots. Note the flattened head and dark-spotted fins.

## SUCKERS

Suckers "vacuum" the bottoms of streams and lakes in search of invertebrates. Their toothless mouths are usually located behind the tip of the snout. Lips are fleshy and suckerlike. They spawn in the spring and often move in large schools.

### LONGNOSE SUCKER
*Catostomus catostomus*
to 51 cm (20 in.)

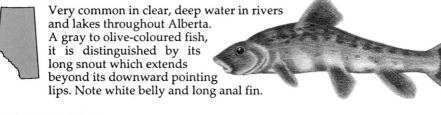

 Very common in clear, deep water in rivers and lakes throughout Alberta. A gray to olive-coloured fish, it is distinguished by its long snout which extends beyond its downward pointing lips. Note white belly and long anal fin.

### WHITE SUCKER
*Catostomus commersoni*
to 56 cm (22 in.)

Common in warm, shallow rivers and lakes. Similar to the Longnose Sucker, it is distinguished by its blunt snout and dark colouration. Despite the name, it ranges in colour from brown and copper to black. Feeds primarily on aquatic invertebrates and insects.

## MINNOWS

These fish are distinguished from similar species by their lack of an adipose fin and toothless jaws. Lips are typically thin, and tail is well forked. Males are generally darker, have red flanks and bellies during spawning season.

### FATHEAD MINNOW
*Pimephales promelas*
to 7 cm (2.5 in.)

 Found in small lakes, ponds, and creeks. Back is brown, sides yellow, and belly silvery. Note dark side stripe. Breeding males develop numerous horny cysts on their snout. Feeds on algae and plankton. A favorite bait fish.

### SPOTTAIL SHINER
*Notropis hudsonius*
to 15cm (6 in.)

Common in lakes, rivers, and streams throughout Alberta. This silvery fish can be distinguished by the small dark spot at the base of its tail. Snout slightly overhangs mouth. Feeds on plankton, algae and insects.

### LAKE CHUB
*Couesius plumbeus*
to 15 cm (6 in.)

Very common in slow-moving streams, rivers, and lakes. A rounded, lead-coloured fish, it resembles a miniature trout. Belly is silvery or white. Males have a red patch at the base of their pectoral fin. Feeds largely on insects and algae.

## TROUT-PERCH

These fish are difficult to classify because it is not known if they are relics of an ancient group, or a highly specialized form of some existing group. Found only in North America, they are exclusively freshwater fishes. They have small mouths and are noted for their peculiarly translucent bodies.

### TROUT-PERCH
*Percopsis omiscomaycus*
to15 cm (6")

Found in large lakes and streams. Seemingly translucent body is silvery-yellow and dark-spotted along the sides. Fins are pale yellow. Note rounded snout and humped back. Feeds on insects and crustaceans.

## COD-LIKE FISHES

A single representative of this bottom-feeding family is found in Alberta. Many have whiskers called "barbels" which are used to detect prey on lake and river bottoms.

### BURBOT
*Lota lota*
to 75 cm (30 in.)

Found in cool waters of lakes and streams throughout Alberta. An elongated, bottom-feeding fish, it is normally a mottled green-gray. Best field marks are the double dorsal fin, and single chin whisker (barbel). Feeds nocturnally on small fish, crustaceans, and insects. Also known as ling cod.

## STICKLEBACKS

These small fish are named for the defined row of spines along their back. Noted for their mating behaviour, the males are responsible for building intricate, suspended nests and guarding the eggs and young.

### BROOK STICKLEBACK
*Culaea inconstans*
to 7 cm (2.5 in.)

Found in shallow streams, pools, and small lakes. Told by slender green body and row of short spines (4-7) ahead of the dorsal fin. Body is dark above, pale below, and mottled on the sides. Feeds on crustaceans, insects, and algae. Its similar cousin, the Ninespine Stickleback, has 7-11 dorsal spines.

## PERCHES

Members of this family are distinguished by their two completely separate dorsal fins and spiny anal fin. The upper jaw protrudes, and the scales have sharp edges.

### YELLOW PERCH
*Perca flavescens*
to 30 cm (12 in.)

Common in lakes and ponds throughout Alberta. Told by its yellow colour, clear eyes, dark side bands, and double dorsal fin. Anal fin usually has two spines. Often travels in schools. Feeds during the day on insects, invertebrates, and small fish.

### SAUGER
*Stizostedion canadense*
to 45 cm (18 in.)

Found primarily in large silty rivers and shallow lakes in southern Alberta. A green-yellow fish, it is told at a glance by its glassy eyes, and double dorsal fin. Distinguished from the Walleye by its black-spotted first dorsal fin and scaled cheeks. Feeds on bottom fauna and small fish.

### WALLEYE
Stizostedion vitreum
*to 82 cm (32 in.)*

Found in lakes and rivers throughout Alberta. Similar to the Sauger, it is distinguished by its larger size, smooth or sparsely scaled cheeks, and unspotted dorsal fins. Note dark blotch at the trailing edge of the first dorsal fin. Often mistakenly referred to as Pickerel, which is a member of the Pike family. Feeds largely on aquatic insects and fish. The Walleye is a prized table fish.

# ALBERTA PLANTS

Based on structural and reproductive characteristics, the plants in this guide can be separated into broad classes of seed plants: the gymnosperms (plants with naked seeds), and the angiosperms (plants with enclosed seeds).

## GYMNOSPERMS - THE NAKED SEED PLANTS

This group of woody, mostly evergreen trees and shrubs include some of the largest and oldest known plants. They began to appear about 350 million years ago in the Devonian period and were the dominant plant species on earth for some 200 million years. The most successful surviving group of gymnosperms is the conifers, which includes such species as pines, spruces, firs, larches and junipers.

The term "gymnosperm" means naked seed, and all members of this group produce naked seeds, usually on the scale of a woody cone. Commonly called "coniferous" or "softwood" trees, most species are evergreen and have small needle-like or scale-like leaves which are adapted to withstand extreme variances in temperature and the abrasions of storms. Some species are deciduous, but most retain their leaves for two or more years before shedding them.

### Reproduction

To better understand the seed method of reproduction, let us look at the life cycle of a pine tree.

Unlike angiosperms, conifers lack flowers or fruits. Pine trees, for example, bear seeds on the inner edge of scale-like leaves which are usually arranged spirally to form a woody cone. Each pine species produces two types of spores, each in a different type of cone (male or female). The spores produced in the male cones develop into winged pollen grains, and these are blown by the wind to eventually fall between the scales of female cones on other trees. The smaller male cones are usually located on the bottom branches of a tree, while the larger female cones are located higher up — probably an adaptation to prevent a tree from pollinating itself. After fertilization, the female spore develops into a seed. When the seed is fully matured, it falls away from the cone and is blown about by the wind. If it reaches favourable ground in proper conditions, it germinates. In pines, it takes as much as a year between pollination and fertilization, and several years may elapse after fertilization until the seeds are shed.

## ANGIOSPERMS - THE FLOWERING PLANTS

Angiosperms first appeared in the fossil record about 130 million years ago. Over the next 60 million years they adapted to various growing conditions, and by the end of the Cretaceous Period (see *Geological Time Scale*, p. 17) they had succeeded gymnosperms as the dominant land plants. Their reproductive success

was largely owing to two key adaptations:
1. They produced flowers to aid in pollen dispersal,
2. They produced seeds encased in "fruits", to aid in seed dispersal.

Angiosperms make up a diverse and widespread group of flowering plants ranging from trees and shrubs like the oaks, cherries, maples, hazelnuts, and apples, to the more typical "flowers" like lilies, orchids, roses, daisies, and violets. Together they provide us with much of our food and shelter, and add colour and aroma to a vast array of settings. The trees and shrubs within this group are commonly called deciduous, broadleaf, or hardwoods, and all shed their leaves annually.

## Reproduction

The reproductive structures of angiosperms are flowers. Flowers are simply modified stems which have evolved into alluring structures for attracting pollinating agents such as bees. Some have even evolved to the point where they attract specific kinds of insects.

A typical flower consists of four sets of leaves attached to the expanded end of the stem, called the receptacle. The outermost leaves, usually green and leaf-like, are called sepals. The often showy, colourful leaves above the sepals which attract insects and birds to aid in pollination are called petals. In flowers which lack petals, the sepals may be colourful and petal-like.

Inside the petals are the male parts of the flower, the stamens. Stamens are composed of the pollen-containing anther which is supported by a thin filament. In the centre of the flower is the female reproductive structure, the pistil. The pistil is composed of a swollen, hollow basal part called the ovary, a narrow neck called the style, and the opening in the style called the stigma. Fertilization occurs when pollen, carried by the wind, insects or animals reaches the ovary. After fertilization, the ovule(s) within the ovary mature into seeds.

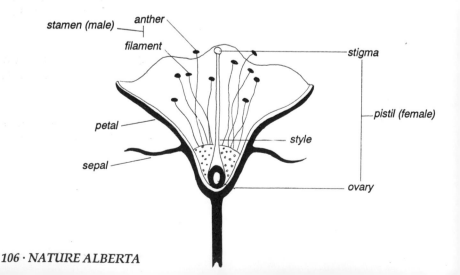

It is important to note that angiosperms vary greatly between species with regard to the shape, position, and number of different parts. Flowers having both stamens and pistils are referred to as perfect flowers. Those which lack organs of one sex are referred to as imperfect flowers.

Once the ovary of a flower becomes fertilized, it begins to develop into a fruit. At this point the sepals, petals, stamens, and style usually fall off. As the fruit matures, the ovules, or seeds, mature; the fruit will contain as many seeds as there were ovules in the ovary. Each seed within itself contains an embryo and a food supply to nourish it upon germination. Upon ripening, the fruit may fall to the ground with the seeds still inside it (as do peaches, cherries and squash), or it may burst open and scatter its seeds in the wind (like poplar trees, pussy willows and dandelions).

Fruit comes in many forms from fleshy berries, grapes, apples, and pears, to pea and bean pods, nuts, burrs, capsules, tomatoes and kernels. The fruit enhances the reproductive success of angiospems in two important ways. First, it helps to protect the seeds from the elements until they have fully matured, enabling the species to survive unfavourable conditions (like winter). Secondly it aids in seed dispersal. Some fruits are eaten by animals and released at other locations, unharmed, in their feces. (Because fruits do not ripen until the seeds are fully matured, animals are discouraged from eating the fruit until the seeds are able to germinate.) Others may be spiny or burred so they catch on the coats of animals, or may have special features which enable them to be carried away from their parent plant by the wind or water.

Angiosperms have evolved into two subclasses — Monocotyledonae and Dicotyledonae — which differ in stem and leaf anatomy, embryonic leaf structure and flower form. Simply put, the monocots make up most cereal plants like wheat, rice, barley and corn, in addition to grasses, lilies and irises. Dicots generally comprise most fruit and vegetables like tomatoes, beans, potatoes and carrots, in addition to willows, maples, elms, buttercups and dandelions. Most of the plants discussed in this field guide are dicots. Each group can be compared and contrasted according to the following features:

**Monocots** - one embryonic leaf at germination, parallel-veined leaves, flower parts (e.g., petals, sepals and stamens) occur in threes or multiples of three, stem is composed of irregularly distributed fibres.

**Dicots** - two embryonic leaves at germination, net-veined leaves, flower parts occur in fours, fives or multiples of these, stem is composed of uniformly distributed fibres, forming rings in many cases.

# ALBERTA TREES

Trees can be broadly defined as perennial woody plants at least 5 metres (16 feet) tall which have a single stem and a well-developed crown of branches, twigs and leaves. Most are long-lived plants ranging in age from 40-50 years for small deciduous trees, to several hundred years for many of the conifers.

The size and shape of a tree is largely determined by its genetic makeup, but its growth is also affected by environmental factors such as moisture, light, and competition from other species. Trees growing in crowded stands will often only support compact crowns, owing to competition for light. Some species like the Whitebark Pine (*Pinus albicaulis* ) grow gnarled and twisted in the mountains owing to the short growing season and constant exposure to high winds.

## HOW TO IDENTIFY TREES

First, note the tree's size and shape. Many trees have characteristic shapes and can be distinguished from a distance by their silhouettes. Next, note the colour and texture of the bark and the arrangement of the twigs. Examine the size, colour, and shape of the leaves and how they are arranged on the twigs. Are they opposite or alternate? Simple or compound? Hairy or smooth? Are flowers or fruits visible on the upper branches? Once you've collected as much information as possible, consult the illustrations and text to determine the family and genus.

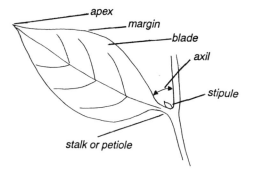

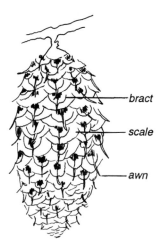

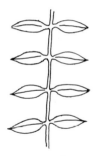  

*opposite*    *alternate*    *whorl*    *basal*

**LEAF ARRANGEMENT**

*scalloped*    *regularly toothed*    *irregularly toothed*

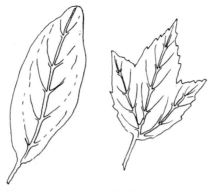

*entire*    *lobed*

**LEAF MARGIN CHARACTERISTICS**

## PINES

The trees and shrubs in this group of evergreens are common throughout Alberta. Most are resin-bearing and have long needle-like leaves which are grouped together in bundles. Male and female cones usually occur on the same tree. Commercially important, they are responsible for the majority of the lumber, pulp, and paper produced in the province. Many are valuable sources of food and cover for wildlife.

### WHITE-BARK PINE
*Pinus albicaulis*
3-10 m  (10-33 ft.)

A small alpine tree found on rocky soil at high altitudes in the southern Rockies. Short, stout trunk supports an irregular crown of spreading branches. Bark is gray and deeply furrowed in mature trees. Stiff needles occur in clusters of five and are densely packed at the end of twigs. The scales of its oval, purple-brown cones (3-5 cm long) are armed with a hard point on each tip. Grows prostrate in exposed locations.

### LIMBER PINE
*Pinus flexilis*
7-15 m  (25-50 ft.)

Common on rocky soil in the mountains and foothills, and on prairie grasslands along the Oldman River. Crown is ragged, and branches tend to grow with their tips upturned. Needles occur in stiff bundles of five and are crowded near the ends of branches. Short-stalked cones (8-20 cm long) have thick scales. Named for its flexible, tough twigs. Grows prostrate on exposed slopes.

## WESTERN WHITE PINE
*Pinus monticola*
15-50 m (50-160 ft.)

Found in the southern mountains at middle and upper elevations. Conical crown of horizontally growing branches is often open and ragged. Long blue-green needles (5-13 cm) are arranged in clusters of five. Slender, long-stalked cones are gently curved toward the tip.

## JACK PINE
*Pinus banksiana*
5-20 m (16-66 ft.)

Found on sandy and rocky soils in central and northern Alberta. Red-brown bark is furrowed into scaly ridges on mature trees. Stiff dark green needles (2-5 cm) are clustered in twos. Distinctive cones are strongly curved and tapered toward the tip. Cone scales bear a sharp spine at their tip. Prevalent in burned-out areas, its cones are stimulated to open during forest fires.

## LODGEPOLE PINE
*Pinus contorta* var. *latifolia*
20-30 m (65-100 ft.)

This is the most common tree on the rocky and sandy soil of the Rockies' slopes. Crown is ragged, and slender trunk is often barren when shaded. Trees growing on the margins of boggy areas are shorter and more shrub-like in appearance. Stiff needles (2-5 cm) are twisted in bundles of two. Gently curved cones grow upward, rather than spreading. Cone scales have a single prickle near their outer edge. It is named for its straight narrow trunk which Indians used as teepee poles.

## LARCHES

Unlike most conifers, larches are deciduous and shed their needles in the fall. Needles grow from woody pegs along twigs in large clusters of 10-40. Cones grow away from branches, often upright, and are usually retained for more than one year. Larches can easily be distinguished from other conifers in autumn by their yellow-gold needles.

## ALPINE LARCH
*Larix lyallii*
to 12 m (40 ft.)

Found on dry soils at high mountain elevations near the treeline. Four-sided, blue-green needles grow in large clusters of 20-40. Distinctive cones have hair-like bracts extending beyond their scale margins. Drooping branches often grow upward at their tip.

## TAMARACK
*Larix laricina*
6-20 m (20-65 ft.)

Found in moist, swampy areas, it is a common muskeg tree in northern Alberta. The irregular crown is composed of slender, spreading branches. Red-brown bark is furrowed and scaly on mature trees. Soft, three-sided needles occur in clusters of 12-20. Small cones (up to 3 cm) are shed after a year. It often grows shrub-like at high elevations.

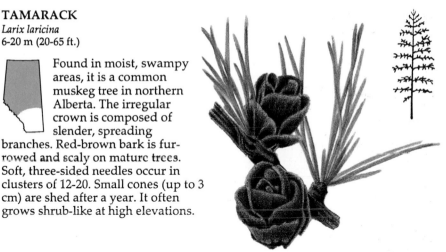

## SPRUCES

These relatively large evergreens are commonly found on moist soils. Clusters of four-sided needles grow from woody pegs along the branches. Hanging cones often grow in clusters.

## BLACK SPRUCE
*Picea mariana*
7-18 m (24-60 ft.)

One of the most common muskeg trees. Slender trunk supports narrow crown which tends to grow in clumps. Drooping branches often grow upwards at their tips. Hairy branchlets are densely covered with stiff, blue-green needles (1-2 cm) which are four-sided and blunt-tipped. Cone scales are rough near their outer edges.

## WHITE SPRUCE
*Picea glauca*
7-30 m (24-100 ft.)

Common throughout much of the province. Tall, straight trunk supports uniform crown of spreading branches. Gray-brown bark is often blistered by resin. Blue-green needles are sharply pointed, and exude a skunky odor when crushed. Hard cylindrical cones have stiff scales with smooth outer edges.

## ENGELMANN SPRUCE
*Picea engelmannii*
20-40 m (65-130 ft.)

Often grows on the wind-swept foothills and mountains. Long barren trunk supports a compact conical crown. Branchlets are covered with soft hairs. Silvery-green needles have blunt, flattened tips, and exude a pungent odor when crushed. It can be distinguished by its hairy branchlets and soft, flexible cones.

# FIRS

Found in northern and western Alberta, firs are medium-sized evergreens with dense, symmetrical crowns. Bark of young trees is smooth and often blistered by resin; mature bark is furrowed and scaly. Flattened, stalkless needles grow singly and bear a longitudinal scar from base to tip. Cones grow upright from branches and disintegrate when seeds are ripe. After the cone scales are shed, a central, candle-like stalk remains on the branch.

## BALSAM FIR
*Abies balsamea*
to 18 m (60 ft.)

Common on moist soils in northeastern Alberta. Uniform crown is pointed at its tip. Flattened needle-like leaves have shiny green surfaces and whitish undersides. Cylindrical purple cones (5-10 cm) grow erect.

## SUBALPINE FIR
*Abies lasiocarpa*
to 10-25 m (33-82 ft.)

Common in alpine forests, it also ranges into west-central Alberta. Uniform conical crown has short, thick branches. Dark green needles have silvery lines on both surfaces and are flattened on lower branches. Cylindrical cones grow erect and have fan-shaped scales. Exposed trees are often low and gnarled, and may appear hedge-like if lower branches take root.

## CEDARS

The Alberta members of this family are primarily junipers. All have scaly or awl-shaped leaves tightly bunched together on twigs. The heavily weighted twigs usually droop at their tips, and give the plants a relaxed profile. Their wood is very fragrant. Unlike cedars and other evergreens, junipers disperse seeds in berry-like, fleshy cones. These resinous, bitter berries are often used to flavor gin.

### GROUND JUNIPER
*Juniperus communis*
to 1.5 m (5 ft.)

This low, mat-forming plant has the widest distribution of any tree or shrub in the northern hemisphere. Common on rocky soil along forest margins and open slopes. Spreading, needle-like leaves are green below, white above, and occur in three's. Berry-like cones are dark blue with a pale bloom. Varieties of this species are commonly used in landscape planting.

### CREEPING JUNIPER
*Juniperus horizontalis*
to 3 m (11 ft.)

A low, spreading shrub which commonly carpets dry areas . Main stems are long and gnarled, giving rise to smaller, variable branchlets. Blue-green leaves may be either awl-shaped (young) or needle-like (mature). Blue cones grow at the ends of branchlets.

## ROCKY MOUNTAIN JUNIPER
*Juniperus scopulorum*
1-3 m (3-11 ft.)

Small tree or upright shrub found on rocky slopes in the southern mountains. May have one or several stems. Leaves are variable and may be either needle-like (young) or scale-like (mature). Cones are bright blue with a pale bloom.

## WILLOWS

While the majority of Alberta willows are shrubs or shrub-like trees, a few reach tree size. Most have narrow, finely toothed leaves which grow alternately along twigs. In spring, flowers often appear before the leaves on semi-erect catkins. After pollination, flowers are succeeded by small pods. When ripe, these pods burst open and shed numerous cottony seeds in the wind. Noted for their extensive root systems, willows are often instrumental in preventing soil erosion along streambanks. For shrub-like willows, see the following section on shrubs.

## BEBB'S WILLOW
*Salix bebbiana*
1-5 m (3-16 ft.)

One of the commonest Alberta willows, it is found in mixed woods and along rivers and lakes. Its wide leaves (1-2.5 cm), are light green above, white below, prominently veined, and sparsely toothed or lacking teeth.

## PUSSY WILLOW
*Salix discolor*
2-5 m (6-16 ft.)

A familiar small tree or shrub found in wet woodlands and bordering sloughs and waterways. One of the earliest flowering willows, it is often found growing in pure stands. Slender leaves (to 10 cm long) are shiny green above, whitish below, and irregularly toothed. Distinctive fuzzy catkins appear in early spring before the leaves (April-May). Red-brown branches are slender and smooth; branchlets are light brown and hairy.

## SCOULER WILLOW
*Salix scouleriana*
1-6 m (3-20 ft.)

A small tree or shrub found in a wide range of habitats throughout Alberta. Straight trunk supports a rounded crown. Blunt-tipped leaves are dark green above, red and woolly below, and widest beyond their middle. Branches are brown to yellow-brown and often covered with fine hairs.

## WEEPING WILLOW
*Salix babylonica*
9-12 m (3-40 ft.)

Native to China, this introduced willow is widely planted as an ornamental throughout Alberta. Easily distinguished by its short trunk and wide crown of drooping (weeping) branches. Narrow, finely toothed leaves are evident from early spring till late autumn.

# POPLARS

Found in moist habitats, these fast-growing trees are common throughout most of the province. Distinguished from willows at a glance by their drooping catkins. Alternate, unlobed leaves are toothed, generally heart-shaped, and usually as long as they are broad. Green-white bark of young trees becomes gray and furrowed as it matures.

## TREMBLING ASPEN
*Populus tremuloides*
to 30 m (100 ft.)

Very common on a variety of soils throughout Alberta. Long, slender trunk supports a compact rounded crown of spreading branches. Rounded leaves have green surfaces, silvery undersides, and are finely toothed. Leaf stalks are usually longer than the leaves themselves. Green white bark becomes riddled with black, wart-like marks as it ages. Its twigs, leaves, catkins and bark are an important food source to several animal and bird species throughout the year. Named for its long-stemmed leaves which quiver in the slightest breeze.

## BALSAM POPLAR
*Populus balsamifera*
to 25 m (80 ft.)

Common and widespread throughout Alberta on moist soils. Long trunk supports a broad crown of ascending branches. Its dark green, leaves are oval to heart-shaped, finely toothed, and have unusually long stems. Bark on mature trees is gray and deeply furrowed, forming rough, flat-topped ridges on the trunk. Branches are gray-brown.

## NARROWLEAF COTTONWOOD
*Populus augustifolia*
to 12 m (40 ft.)

 A slender tree found in moist soil along rivers and streams in southern Alberta. Distinguished from similar species by its ascending branches, narrow crown, and slender, willow-like leaves. Green-white bark becomes slightly furrowed in mature trees.

## BIRCHES

Most members of this family occur as shrubs in Alberta. In all, the male and female flowers occur in catkins on the same plant. Alternate leaves are commonly oval-shaped with prominently toothed margins. The cylindrical cones disintegrate in the fall when ripe. Fruit is either a winged nutlet or a nut enclosed in a leafy case. All are fast growing.

## PAPER BIRCH
*Betula papyrifera*
to 25 m (80 ft.)

 Common on moist soil in forested regions of Alberta. Straight trunk supports a rounded to conical crown of ascending branches. Dull green leaves are irregularly toothed (except near their base) and have 5-9 straight side veins. Smooth bark is whitish to red-brown, and peels off easily in thin sheets. Thrives in burned-out and cut-over areas where it quickly reproduces by suckering. Indians used to use birch bark to construct light-weight canoes because of its pliability.

# MAPLES

Alberta unfortunately has few representatives of this distinctive and well-known family. Maples are distinguished by their large, opposite leaves, and long-winged seed pairs. The leaves are especially conspicuous in autumn when they turn vivid shades of orange and red before falling off. Alberta's maples do not produce usable syrup.

## DOUGLAS MAPLE
*Acer glabrum* var. *douglasii*
to 10 m (33 ft.)

Shrub or small tree commonly found in moist locations along streams and sheltered slopes in the mountains and foothills. Most occur as small shrubs with short trunks and irregular crowns. Opposite leaves have 3-5 lobes, reddish stems, and saw-toothed edges. Winged seed pairs are green or pink on the tree, turning brown in autumn. Smooth bark is red-brown to gray.

# ALBERTA SHRUBS

Shrubs are perennial woody plants, normally less than 5 metres (16 in.) tall which support a crown of branches, twigs and leaves. Unlike trees they are anchored to the ground by several stems, rather than by a single trunk. Most are fast-growing and are an important source of food and shelter for wildlife.

## HOW TO IDENTIFY SHRUBS

The species in the shrub section have been arranged by berry colour rather than family in order to facilitate field identification. For those who are interested, the family name of each species can be found in the *Checklists* in the back of the book.

For ease of identification, shrubs have been grouped into four general colour categories:

- shrubs with reddish berries
- shrubs with bluish berries
- shrubs with whitish berries
- shrubs lacking berries

Even experts often find it difficult to indentify shrubs in the wild, and it is hoped that keying on berry colour will give the novice a fighting chance when the berries are present. It is important to remember, however, that berries are seasonal. When berries are absent, try noting leaf and structural characteristics in order to make an identification.

As with trees, important features to consider are twigs, bark, flowers, fruit, buds and location.

## SHRUBS WITH REDDISH BERRIES

### NORTHERN GOOSEBERRY
*Ribes oxyacanthoides* (Gooseberry Family)
to 120 cm (4 ft.)

A low, erect shrub found in moist woodlands and along watercourses. Leaves are thorned near their base and grow on prickly branches. Green, tubular flowers appear in early spring. These are succeeded by green berries, which redden as they mature.

### PIN CHERRY
*Prunus pensylvanica* (Rose Family)
3-8 m (10-25 ft.)

A shrub or small tree common on moist soils in wooded and open areas. Straight trunk supports a narrow to rounded crown of spreading branches. Alternate, narrow leaves are pointed and finely toothed. White flowers have orange-banded throats and bloom in clusters of four to five in May-June. Yellow-tipped stamens project well beyond the petal margin. The bitter red berry has a large pit.

### RED CHOKE CHERRY
*Prunus virginiana* (Rose Family)
2-6 m (6-20 ft.)

A bushy shrub or tree found along streams, wooded margins, and brushy slopes. Its trunk is often twisted. Red-gray bark smells bitter when bruised. Light green, alternate leaves are smooth-sided and sharply toothed. Spring flowers bloom in long cylindrical clusters between May and June. Berries are dark red-purple when mature.

### WILD RED RASPBERRY
*Rubus idaeus* (Rose Family)
to 150 cm (60 in.)

Common along roadsides, streams, and forest margins. The compound leaves are evenly toothed and hairy beneath. Main stems and branches are covered in small prickles. White flowers bloom in June-July. Bright red raspberry fruits appear in late summer.

### EUROPEAN MOUNTAIN ASH
*Sorbus aucuparia* (Rose Family)
to 10 m (33 ft.)

A common shrub or tree, this introduced species is widely planted as an ornamental throughout the province. Short trunk supports an open crown of spreading branches. Alternate, compound leaves have 9-15 leaflets and are bluntly toothed. White flowers bloom in dense clusters in early spring; these are succeeded by the familiar flattened clusters of red berries which persist into winter. Winter buds are covered with a coat of fine white hairs. Its berries are a favourite food of waxwings.

### CANADIAN BUFFALO-BERRY
*Shepherdia canadensis* (Oleaster Family)
2-4 m (6-12 ft.)

Sprawling shrub common throughout the forest regions of Alberta. Leaves have waxy green surfaces and silvery, brown-spotted undersides. Small clusters of yellow flowers bloom along leafy stems in May-June. Juicy red berries succeed the flowers in early summer.

## LOW-BUSH CRANBERRY
*Viburnum edule* (Honeysuckle Family)
70-200 cm (2-6 ft.)

Common in moist woodlands throughout the province. Leaves are three-lobed, deeply veined, and hairy underneath. White flowers bloom in June and are densely clustered at the tips of branches. Bright red berries appear in summer. The similar High-bush Cranberry can be distinguished by its larger size (to 4 metres high), and more deeply lobed leaves.

## TWINING HONEYSUCKLE
*Lonicera glaucescens* (Honeysuckle Family)
1-2 m (2-6 ft.)

A vine-like plant found twining through shrubs in moist open woodlands. Opposite leaves are oval-shaped, and two or more are usually joined beneath flower clusters. Its clusters of showy, yellow tubular flowers are excellent summer field mark. Fall berries are red. Honeysuckles are commonly planted as ornamentals.

## SHRUBS WITH BLUISH BERRIES

## WILD BLACK CURRANT
*Ribes hudsonianum* (Gooseberry Family)
1-1.5 m (3-5 ft.)

An erect, branching shrub found in moist woods and thickets throughout Alberta. Alternate leaves are toothed and have 3-5 lobes. Small, tassel-like, white flowers bloom in drooping clusters in May. These are succeeded by red berries which blacken as they mature. One of seven species of currants native to Alberta.

## SASKATOON SERVICEBERRY
*Amelanchier alnifolia* (Rose Family)
1-6 m (3-20 ft.)

Also called Western Serviceberry, it is common in moist valleys and open wooded areas throughout the province. A shrub or small tree, it often grows in dense thickets. Alternate, leathery leaves are coarsely toothed above the middle. White, star-shaped spring flowers bloom in multiple clusters at the ends of branchlets in June. Juicy, purple-black berries appear in early summer.

## DWARF BLUEBERRY
*Vaccinium caespitosum* (Heath Family)
to 30 cm (12 ft.)

A dense, low-growing shrub common on poor soil in open coniferous forests. Dark green leaves have shiny surfaces and downy undersides. Pink-white flowers bloom in June-July. Edible blue berries appear in August. One of five species of blueberry found in Alberta.

## BRACTED HONEYSUCKLE
*Lonicera involucrata* (Honeysuckle Family)
30-100 cm (1-3 ft.)

An erect, low-growing shrub commonly found on moist soil in open woodlands and meadows. Opposite oval leaves are deeply veined. Paired yellow flowers bloom in July and have distinctive short leaves (bracts) at their base. As the purple-black berries appear, the bracts change colour from green to red.

## BUCKBRUSH
*Symphoricarpos occidentalis* (Honeysuckle Family)
30-120 cm (1-4 ft.)

Found throughout the province on dry soil in open areas. Opposite leathery leaves are hairy underneath and often toothed. Pink bell-shaped flowers bloom in small clusters at the end of branchlets in July. Waxy white berries turn purplish with age.

SHRUBS WITH WHITISH BERRIES

## SILVERBERRY
*Elaeagnus commutata* (Oleaster Family)
1-4 m (3-13 ft.)

An erect shrub common on dry soil on fields and hillsides throughout Alberta. Stiff curled leaves have a shiny, silvery surface. Yellow flowers bloom in June-July in small clusters along stems. These are succeeded by tough silvery berries containing a single seed. Also referred to as Wolf Willow.

## RED OSIER DOGWOOD
*Cornus stolonifera* (Dogwood Family)
1-2 m (3-6 ft.)

A sprawling, thicket-forming shrub common in forests, moist meadows, and along waterways and roadsides. Opposite leaves have sunken veins and red stalks. Green-white flowers bloom in dense flattened clusters in June. Waxy white berries appear in late summer. Bright red bark is an excellent field mark throughout the year.

## SNOWBERRY
*Symphoricarpos albus* (Honeysuckle Family)
1-4 m (3-13 ft.)

A low, spreading shrub commonly found in wooded areas. Thin leaves are usually coarsely toothed and have hairy undersides. Pink, bell-shaped flowers bloom in clusters near the end of twigs in early summer. These are succeeded by waxy, white berries that persist into early winter.

## SANDBAR WILLOW
*Salix exigua* (Willow Family)
to 4 m (13 ft.)

A thicket-forming shrub or small tree found on sandy soil along stream and river banks. Narrow yellow-green leaves (3-9 mm wide) are long, slightly curved, and downy beneath. Branches and leaf stems are red-brown in colour.

## BEAKED HAZELNUT
*Corylus cornuta* (Birch Family)
1-3 m (3-10 ft.)

A bushy, erect shrub commonly found growing in clumps in open woodlands. Alternate leaves have sharply toothed margins and are hairy beneath along the veins. Inconspicuous pink flowers and hanging yellow catkins appear in spring before the leaves. Nut-like fruits mature within hairy, leafy sheaths, and ripen into edible filberts by autumn.

## SHRUBS LACKING BERRIES

### WATER BIRCH
*Betula occidentalis* (Birch Family)
to 10 m (33 ft.)

Shrub or small tree found along the margins of lakes and streams throughout the province. Short trunk supports an irregular crown of slender, upright branches. Oval, green-yellow leaves have sharply saw-toothed edges and smooth bases. Shiny red-brown bark is horizontally streaked with small pores, and does not peel as easily as bark of other birch species. Brown, papery catkins disintegrate in summer when seeds are ripe.

### GREEN ALDER
*Alnus crispa* (Birch Family)
to 3 m (10 ft.)

An erect shrub found in moist, wooded areas in the northern half of the province. Shiny leaves have sharply toothed edges and do not change colour in fall. Green catkins appear in summer and mature into small, woody cone-like fruits by autumn.

### MOUNTAIN ALDER
*Alnus tenuifolia* (Birch Family)
to 7 m (23 ft.)

Large shrub or small tree commonly found on moist soil bordering swamps, streams, and lakes. Bark on mature branches is red-orange and smooth. Alternate dark green leaves are sharply serrated and have an orangish central vein. Woody cone-like fruits appear in fall and remain on the shrub until the following summer.

# ALBERTA WILDFLOWERS

Wildflowers are soft-stemmed flowering plants, smaller than trees or shrubs, which grow anew each year. Some regenerate annually from the same rootstock (perennials), while others grow from seeds and last a single season (annuals). Most have flowering stems bearing colourful blossoms which ripen into fruits as the growing season progresses. Their flowering stems typically grow upright, but may be climbing, creeping or trailing. They range from weeds and reeds to roses and buttercups, and are found almost everywhere. From the cracks in city sidewalks, to mountain meadows, to the parched prairies, wildflowers are abundant and widespread throughout Alberta.

(For a detailed look at flowers and how they reproduce, refer to the discussion on angiosperms at the beginning of the plant section.)

## HOW TO IDENTIFY WILDFLOWERS

The species in the wildflower section have been arranged in the following colour groups rather than family in order to facilitate field identificartion:

- · White
- · Yellow and Green
- · Red, Pink and Orange
- · Blue and Purple

For those who are interested, the family name of each species can be found in the *Checklists* in the back of the book.

After noting colour, examine the shape of the flower heads. Are they daisy-like, bell-shaped, or odd in appearance? How are they arranged on the plant? Do they occur singly, or in rounded or elongated clusters? Pay close attention to the leaves and how they are arranged on the stem. When you think you know what the plant might be, refer to the text to confirm its size, habitat, and blooming period (N.B. — the blooming periods of flowers can vary year by year depending on the weather. The dates given are meant to serve as general guidelines).

Remember that flowers are wildlife and should be treated as such. Many species have been seriously depleted because of loss of habitat and over-picking; in many areas, once-abundant species are now rare. You can learn as much about a wildflower in the field as by bringing it home since they are so easy to observe. Bring along a sketchbook and camera and record the flowers without picking them. This will help ensure there are more blossoms for others to enjoy next year.

The following drawings illustrate the different possible arrangements of multiple flowerheads on a stem.

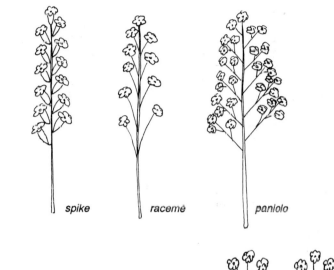

spike     raceme     paniolo

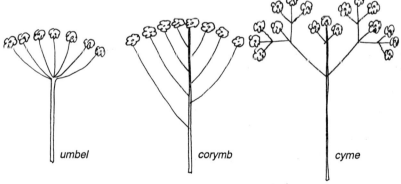

umbel     corymb     cyme

## FAIRY BELLS
*Disporum trachycarpum* (Lily Family)
to 76 cm (30 in.)

Common in moist wooded areas. Stalkless leaves have crinkled edges and grow along the entire stem length. Branching stem supports drooping clusters of 1-4 white, bell-shaped flowers. Yellow-tipped stamens normally project beyond the petal margin. Blooms May-June. Flowers are succeeded by bright orange-red berries.

## STAR-FLOWERED SOLOMON'S SEAL
*Smilacina stellata*
20-60 cm (8-24 in.)

Very common throughout the wooded and parkland regions of the province. Numerous leaves with clasping bases are arranged rather stiffly along the kinked stems. Small white flowers are short-lived and borne in open clusters. Blooms June-July.

## FALSE ASPHODEL
*Tofieldia glutinosa* (Lily Family)
to 45 cm (18 in.)

Found in wet woods, ditches, and marshy areas. The 3 or 4 basal leaves are slender and grass-like in appearance. The single, sticky-hairy stem supports a long cluster of small white flowers at its tip. Stamens normally project beyond the petal margin and have conspicuous purplish anthers. Blooms July-August.

## ROUND-LEAVED ORCHID
*Orchis rotundifolia* (Orchid Family)
10-25 cm (4-10 in.)

Common in moist boreal forests and mixed woods throughout Alberta. Shiny pad-like basal leaf is conspicuous at the base of a slender, naked flower stalk. Pink to white orchids bloom in loose terminal spike, and can be distinguished by their purple-spotted lower lips. Blooms June-July.

## RUSSIAN THISTLE
*Salsola kali* var. *tenuifolia* (Goosefoot Family)
to 1 m (39 in.)

A very common introduced weed found on dry soils throughout Alberta. Sharply tipped leaves are densely clustered on branching stems. Inconspicuous flowers bloom in long spikes in June-July. At maturity, the entire plant breaks off near the ground, becoming a tumbleweed.

## FIELD CHICKWEED
*Cerastium arvense* (Pink Family)
15-25 cm (6-10 in.)

Common on dry soil in the prairie and parkland regions. Gray-green leaves have silky surfaces and grow densely along semi-prostrate, hairy stems. Showy white flowers bloom in dense clusters between May and June.

## RED AND WHITE BANEBERRY
*Actaea rubra* (Crowfoot Family)
25-100 cm (10-40 in.)

This perennial herb is far more conspicuous when in fruit than in flower. Large compound leaves are deeply saw-toothed and have many pointed leaflets. Long leafy stems support dense, conical crowns of tiny, delicate white flowers. In early autumn the flowers are replaced by red or white, poisonous berries. Blooms May-July. Common in moist forests throughout Alberta.

## CANADA ANEMONE
*Anemone canadensis* (Crowfoot Family)
20-65 cm (8-25 in.)

Abundant in damp, open woodlands and along shorelines. Light green leaves have 3-5 lobes and are sharply serrated. Basal leaves are long-stalked; stem leaves are stalkless. Star-shaped white flowers have 5 petal-like sepals and yellowish centres. Blooms June-July.

## GRASS-OF-PARNASSUS
*Parnassia palustris* var. *neogaea*
(Grass-of-Parnassus Family) to 30 cm (12 in.)

Found in dense colonies in wet mossy areas and along streams. Each stem supports a solitary flower and has a single, stalkless leaf between its middle and base. A cluster of glossy, kidney-shaped leaves spread out from the plant base. Star-shaped white flowers have five green-veined petals. Blooms July-August.

## PENNY CRESS
*Thlaspi arvense* (Mustard Family)
to 50 cm (20 in.)

This introduced plant is very common in fields and waste areas. Leaves are coarsely toothed and clasp the stem along its length. Small white flowers bloom in dense terminal clusters from June to September. Also called Stinkweed, its flowers exude an offensive, camphorous odour.

## WHITE CLOVER
*Trifolium repens* (Legume Family)
to 30 cm (12 in.)

This introduced plant is common in fields, lawns, and waste areas. Long-stemmed, dark green leaves have three oval leaflets, and grow densely along creeping, mat-forming stems. Rounded white flowers bloom May-October. An excellent nectar producer, it is a favourite of bees. Red and Pink Clover (*T. pratense* and *T. hybridium* respectively) are also common in the province.

## WILD WHITE GERANIUM
*Geranium richardsonii* (Geranium Family)
40-100 cm (16-40 in.)

Common in moist woodlands and thickets. Large, bright green leaves have three to seven coarsely toothed lobes, and grow along the entire stem length. The open, pink-white flowers have broad petals which are often pink-veined. Blooms June-September.

## WESTERN CANADA VIOLET
*Viola rugulosa* (Violet Family)
25-50 cm (10-20 in.)

This harbinger of spring is common on rich soil in shady, wooded areas. Numerous heart-shaped leaves grow along the length of the branching stems. White to violet flowers have purple-veined petals and yellow centres. Blooms May-August. Often found in dense colonies.

## COW PARSNIP
*Heracleum lanatum* (Parsley Family)
1-2 m (40-80 in.)

This large, conspicuous plant is very common in moist fields and woods. Large, deeply lobed leaves grow along the length of its thick, hollow stem. Dense flattened clusters of creamy white flowers bloom between June and August. Though non-poisonous, it resembles similar plants, like the Water Hemlock, which are deadly.

## BUNCHBERRY
*Cornus canadensis* (Dogwood Family)
7-15 cm (3-6 in.)

A mat-forming herb common in moist woods and bogs throughout the province. Stems arise from a creeping rootstock which runs underground. Each plant has a whorl of 4-6 oval-shaped leaves and what appears to be a single large, white flower. The 4 petal-like lobes of the flower are actually bracts which surround a small cluster of green-yellow flowers. Bright red berries succeed the flowers in late summer. Blooms June-July.

## LABRADOR TEA
*Ledum groenlandicum* (Heath Family)
30-100 cm (1-3 ft.)

A shrub common in moist coniferous forests. Erect, reddish stems are finely haired. The narrow, leathery leaves are red and woolly below, and have rolled margins. Clusters of small white flowers bloom at stem tips in June-July. The leaves have been used as a tea substitute since the times of the early settlers.

## FAIRY CANDELABRA
*Androsace septentrionalis* (Primrose Family)
to 25 cm (10 in.)

This small, delicate plant is very common on dry fields in southern Alberta. Stems arise from a leafy base and branch at tips to support tiny primrose-like flowers. The fragrant flowers are creamy white with a yellow or pink centre. Blooms April-May.

## BUCK-BEAN
*Menyanthes trifoliata* (Gentian Family)
to 20 cm (8 in.)

This low-growing plant is found in ditches and boggy areas. Thick, compound leaves have three rounded, toothless leaflets. Its tubular white flowers have glistening hairs on their upper surface and appear feathery. Flowers and leaves arise from a thick, creeping stem. Blooms June-July.

### WILD MORNING GLORY
*Convolvulus sepium* (Morning-glory Family)
A climbing vine.

An introduced weed common in fields, thickets, and waste areas. A twining, climbing plant; its stems may be up to 3 metres long. Triangular leaves and wide-mouthed, whitish-pink flowers occur at intervals along the stem. Blooms May-August.

### MOSS PHLOX
*Phlox hoodii* (Phlox Family)
to 5 cm (2 in.)

A mat-forming plant common on open prairies and eroded areas in southern Alberta. Tiny, narrow leaves (to 10 mm long) grow crowded along creeping stems, forming a dense green base. Conspicuous clusters of white, yellow-centred flowers with 5 lobes bloom in March-June.

### COMMON PLANTAIN
*Plantago major* (Plantain Family)
to 50 cm

An introduced species very common in lawns, gardens, and waste areas throughout the province. Large, tough basal leaves are finely toothed with deep longitudinal veins. Tiny greenish flowers bloom in slender spikes between June-August.

## NORTHERN BEDSTRAW
*Galium boreale* (Madder Family)
20-70 cm (8-28 in.)

Very common in moist woods, meadows, and along roadsides throughout Alberta. Narrow leaves grow in whorls of four along slender, four-sided stem. Dense clusters of tiny, cross-shaped, white flowers bloom in terminal clusters in July-August. These abundant, fragrant plants were once used as mattress stuffing.

## ARROW-LEAVED COLTSFOOT
*Petasites sagittatus* (Composite Family)
to 30 cm (12 in.)

Common and widespread in moist woodlands and boggy areas. Arrow-shaped basal leaves are gray-green above, white and hairy below. Tiny white flowers bloom in dense terminal clusters in May-June. These are quickly succeeded by tufts of cottony seeds which resemble small cotton balls.

## COMMON YARROW
*Achillea millefolium* (Composite Family)
to 60 cm (24 in.)

Common in ditches, fields, and waste areas in southern Alberta. The unusual fern-like leaves are a good field mark. Its long, branching stem supports dense flattened clusters of small daisy-like flowers. Each flower has 4-6 white (occasionally pink) rays. Blooms June-August.

### YELLOW AND GREEN FLOWERS

## COMMON CATTAIL
*Typha latifolia* (Cattail Family)
1-3 m (3-10 ft.)

This aquatic plant is common in marshes, ditches, and along lakes and rivers throughout the province. Familiar to most, it can be distinguished by its prominent club-like sheath of greenish flower spikes atop a long stalk. The flowers ripen into brownish tufts of hairy seeds in late summer, giving the plant its characteristic appearance.

## GLACIER LILY
*Erythronium grandiflorum* (Lily Family)
20-40 cm (8-16 in.)

Found in open meadows and moist woods in the foothills and mountains. Two large, slender leaves arise from the plant base. The naked flower stalk supports a large, bright yellow, nodding flower. As the plant matures, the pointed petals gently fold back to expose the pistil and stamens. Blooms March-June (depending on elevation). One of the first flowers to bloom in spring, it often appears before the snow has completely melted.

## WHITE CAMAS
*Zygadenus elegans*
30-60 cm (12-25 in.)

Common in many different areas throughout the foothills and mountains. Grass-like leaves are mostly basal and are keeled along their midrib. Small lily-like greenish-white flowers bloom in an open cluster at the end of the flowering stalk. The bulb of this perennial is poisonous to livestock. Blooms July-August.

## YELLOW LADY'S SLIPPER
*Cypripedium calceolus* var. *pubescens*
(Orchid Family) 15-45 cm (6-18 in.)

Found in moist forests and
boggy areas throughout Alberta.
Prominently veined leaves are
somewhat hairy and clasp the
stem. Bright yellow, pouch-like
flowers are elegantly framed by
spirally twisted yellow or brown petals.
Blooms June-July. Often found growing
in clumps, it is one of our most common
orchids.

## NORTHERN GREEN BOG ORCHID
*Habenaria hyperborea* (Orchid Family)
15-60 cm (6-24 in.)

Found in bogs, marshes, and
damp woods throughout
Alberta. Slender leaves clasp the
stem, and are larger towards the
plant base. A narrow cluster of
small green orchids are crowded
near the tip of the stem. Related to six
similar species. Blooms June-August.

## COMMON NETTLE
*Urtica gracilis* (Nettle Family)
to 2 m (78 in.)

Common in fields, thickets, and
waste areas throughout the
province. Toothed leaves have
sharp prickles that eject a sting-
ing substance on contact. Drooping spikes of green flowers
bloom June-August.

## LAMB'S QUARTERS
*Chenopodium album* (Goosefoot Family)
to 1 m (39 in.)

This familiar, introduced weed is widespread throughout the province. Distinguished by its grooved stalk, numerous branching stems, and dense foliage. Green flowers lack petals and resemble tiny cauliflowers. Blooms June-August.

## YELLOW POND LILY
*Nuphar variegatum* (Water Lily Family)
A floating plant.

Found on surface of sloughs, ponds, and slow-moving streams. Buoyant, leathery leaves, each with a deep V-shaped notch at the base, float on the surface. A bright yellow, bulbous flower blooms among the leaves between June-July. Roots are anchored in the muddy bottom.

## MARSH MARIGOLD
*Caltha palustris* (Crowfoot Family)
20-40 cm (8-16 in.)

Common in wet meadows, swamps, and moist woodlands throughout the province. Rounded, heart-shaped leaves have gently toothed margins. Slender, branching stem supports several bright yellow flowers with 5 to 9 petal-like sepals. One of our earliest bloomers, its succulent leaves are a popular source of spring greens for some. Blooms April-May.

## CREEPING BUTTERCUP
*Ranunculus cymbalaria* (Crowfoot Family)
to 20 cm (8 in.)

Common along the edges of streams and sloughs. A low-growing plant, it spreads over the ground on its branching roots. Its distinctive, rounded, long-stalked leaves are a good field mark. Small yellow flowers bloom atop leafless stems in June-July.

## TALL BUTTERCUP
*Ranunculus acris* (Crowfoot Family)
to 1 m (39 in.)

This introduced plant is very common in wet fields, mead-ows, and along roadside ditches throughout the province. Its large, long-stalked leaves are deeply lobed and sharply serrated. Branching, hairy stem supports several bright yellow, 5-petalled flowers. Blooms June-July.

## VEINY MEADOW RUE
*Thalictrum venulosum* (Crowfoot Family)
15-75 cm (6-30 in.)

Very common in moist mead-ows and woodlands. Unlike most Alberta wildflowers, its male and female flowers occur on separate plants. Compound leaves grow densely along entire length of slender, branching stem. Dense, drooping clusters of tassel-like yellow flowers bloom at stem tips in June-July.

## WILD MUSTARD
*Brassica kaber* (Mustard Family)
25-80 cm (10-32 in.)

An introduced weed very common in fields, ditches, and waste areas. Its alternate leaves are slender and irregularly toothed. Hairy stem supports dense clusters of cross-shaped yellow flowers which bloom between June and July. Each flower has 4 broad yellow petals and 4 green sepals. Related to over 15 similar species.

## YELLOW DRYAD
*Dryas drummondii* (Rose Family)
to 25 cm (10 in.)

Common on rocky soil in the montane and mountain regions. Leathery leaves are shiny green above, white and woolly below. Its leafless, hairy stem rises from a dense mat of low-growing leaves and supports a single nodding yellow flower. Note hairy leaves (sepals) enclosing the flower at its base. Blooms June-August.

## SHRUBBY CINQUEFOIL
*Potentilla fruticosa* (Rose Family)
to 1 m (39 in.)

This erect or spreading shrub is common in a variety of habitats from rocky fields to moist meadows. Its gray-green leaves are divided into 3-7 wedge-shaped leaflets which are slightly hairy with smooth margins. Bright yellow, rose-like flowers bloom from June to September. Because of their long blooming period they are widely planted as ornamentals.

## WHITE PEA VINE
*Lathyrus ochroleucus* (Legume Family)
A climbing plant.

 Common in open woodlands and brushy areas throughout Alberta. Its leaves are divided into 8-12 oval leaflets which are deeply veined. Cream-coloured flowers bloom in clusters of 10-20 along the length of the branching, climbing stem. Blooms May-August.

## EARLY YELLOW LOCOWEED
*Oxytropis sericea* var. *spicata* (Legume Family)
to 60 cm (24 in.)

 Common on prairies and grassy slopes in southern Alberta. Gray green leaves have 7-20 leaflets and grow upward, along with stems, from the plant base. Pale yellow flowers are loosely clustered in a terminal spike. Often grows in thick clusters. Named for the poisonous chemical it contains which, when ingested, appears to cause mental disturbances in livestock. Related to 9 similar species. Blooms May-July.

## PRICKLY PEAR CACTUS
*Opuntia polyacantha* (Cactus Family)
to 50 cm (20 in.)

 This mat-forming cactus is common on dry soil in southern Alberta. Cactus segments are flattened and covered with clusters of sharp, slender spines. Showy yellow flowers have large spreading petals. Blooms June-July.

## YELLOW EVENING PRIMROSE
*Oenothera biennis* (Evening Primrose Family)
1-2 m (3-6 ft.)

Very common on roadsides, fields, and waste areas, it can often be distinguished at a distance by its long, stout stem. Its dark green, lance-shaped leaves are stalked near the bottom of the plant, and stalkless near the top. The bright yellow flowers with 4 petals open in the evening and close in the morning. Blooms July-August.

## YELLOW PUCCOON
*Lithospermum ruderale* (Borage Family)
to 50 cm (20 in.)

Common on grasslands and dry slopes in southern Alberta. Its narrow, stiff leaves are crowded along wiry stems. Small yellow flowers bloom among leaves at stem tips between June-August. Also called Stoneseed, in reference to the hard nutlets the plant produces.

## YELLOW TOAD FLAX
*Linaria vulgaris* (Figwort Family)
20-80 cm (8-32 in.)

An introduced plant common in fields and waste areas throughout Alberta. The gray-green leaves are narrow, stalkless, and grow along the length of the stem. Yellow flowers bloom in a long terminal cluster; each has a long, tapered spur, and a prominent orange pouch on its lower lip. Blooms June-July. Also referred to as Butter-and-Eggs.

## WESTERN LOUSEWORT
*Pedicularis bracteosa* (Figwort Family)
40-100 cm (15-40 in.)

Found in moist open woodlands and meadows in the foothills and mountains. Distinctive fern-like leaves and stiff, purple stem are good field marks. Arching tubular flowers are borne in a dense terminal cluster. Yellow flowers and upper leaves are often tinged with purple. Blooms July-August.

## COMMON BLADDERWORT
*Utricularia vulgaris* var. *americana*
(Bladderwort Family) 10-30 cm (4-12 in.)

This aquatic plant is found in sloughs, ditches, and lakes. Buoyant leaves are finely divided and serve to keep the plant afloat. Like all bladderworts, its leaves bear small bladders which trap small aquatic animals to provide the plant with nourishment. Stout, leafless stalks bear clusters of up to 20 yellow flowers. Blooms June-July.

## HEART-LEAVED ARNICA
*Arnica cordifolia* (Composite Family)
30-60 cm (12-24 in.)

Common in open coniferous forests in southern and western Alberta. Leaves are heart-shaped and sharply serrated. Coarse stem supports a bright yellow, daisy-like flower with wide-spreading petals. Related to 14 similar species. Blooms June-August.

### WILD GAILLARDIA
*Gaillardia aristata* (Composite Family)
30-60 cm (12-24 in.)

Common on dry fields and roadsides in southern Alberta. Gray-green leaves are narrow, hairy, and grow along length of branching stems. Distinguished in the field at a glance by its showy yellow, brown-centred flowers. Also referred to as a Brown-eyed Susan. Blooms July-August.

### COMMON DANDELION
*Taraxacum officinale* (Composite Family)
to 30 cm (12 in.)

Abundant in open and grassy areas, this introduced plant is the most widespread weed in the province. A stemless plant, its cut-toothed leaves and flowering stalk arise from a fleshy root. Its bright yellow flowers bloom frequently throughout the growing season. Tufts of whitish, hairy seeds succeed the flowers which are dispersed by the wind. The leaves are commonly used in salads, and the blossoms for wine-making.

### FALSE DANDELION
*Agoseris glauca* (Composite Family)
to 45 cm  (18 in.)

Widely distributed throughout the province in a variety of habitats. Distinguished from the Common Dandelion by its narrow, finely toothed leaves. Both the leaves and flower stalks are gray-green and often hairy. Single yellow flower head blooms atop fleshy stalk between July and August. Mature flowers are often pinkish.

## PRAIRIE CONEFLOWER
*Ratibida columnifera* (Composite Family)
20-60 cm (8-24 in.)

Common on dry soil in the grassland region. Slender, fern-like leaves grow alternately along the stalk. Easily distinguished by its showy, cone-like flower heads surrounded by drooping yellow rays. Blooms July-September.

## TALL SMOOTH GOLDENROD
*Solidago gigantea* (Composite Family)
1-2 m (3-6 in.)

Common in dense colonies on margins of forests and thickets. Long leaves are lance-shaped, toothed, and deeply veined. Clusters of yellow, daisy-like flowers are borne along spreading, recurved branches. Blooms August-September. Numerous similar species are also found in the province.

## ANNUAL SUNFLOWER
*Helianthus annuus* (Composite Family)
1-2 m (3-6 ft.)

Common on roadsides and dry waste areas in southern Alberta. Large oval leaves are hairy and coarsely toothed. Slender stems are covered with short stiff hairs. Large flower head has numerous yellow rays surrounding a dark brown, flattened central disk. Similar to several related species.

## RED, PINK, AND ORANGE FLOWERS

### WESTERN WOOD LILY
*Lilium philadelphicum* var. *andinum* (Lily Family)
20-60 cm (8-24 in.)

 Found in fields, meadows, and open wooded areas throughout Alberta. Lance-shaped leaves point upward, and grow in whorls along the stem. Chalice-shaped orange flowers are the best field mark. The inner edges of the petals are golden and dark-spotted at their base. Blooms June-August. The Western Wood Lily is Saskatchewan's floral emblem.

### NODDING ONION
*Allium cernuum* (Lily Family)
10-50 cm (4-20 in.)

 Found in open woodlands and moist meadows in southern Alberta. Leaves are grass-like and grow upward from the plant base. Its slender flowering stalk supports a large nodding cluster of numerous, pinkish or white bulbous flowers. The entire plant has an onion-like odor. Blooms June-August.

### VENUS' SLIPPER
*Calypso bulbosa* (Orchid Family)
10-20 cm (4-8 in.)

 This beautiful woodland orchid is commonly found in dry woodlands. A single, broad, pointed leaf grows at the plant base. The striking pinkish flower has an inflated, slipper-like, lower lip which often has a white outer edge; the inner surface is streaked and spotted with purple and brown, and features rows of golden yellow hairs. One of our earliest blooming orchids, it is often found in dense colonies. Blooms May-July.

## PRICKLY WILD ROSE
*Rosa acicularis* (Rose Family)
15-60 cm (6-24 in.)

Common in open wooded areas, thickets, and along roadsides. Branches and stems are densely covered with soft prickles. Compound leaves have 5-7 leaflets. Red-pink, yellow-centred flowers bloom June-July. Similar to the Common Wild Rose, it is best distinguished by its leaves. It is Alberta's floral emblem.

## COMMON WILD ROSE
*Rosa Woodsii* (Rose Family)
30-150 cm (1-5 ft.)

The most abundant and widespread rose in the province, it is common in forested areas and fields. Compound leaves have 5-9 leaflets which are hairy below. Stems are stout and prickly. Deep pink, yellow-centred flowers bloom June-July.

## OLD MAN'S WHISKERS
*Geum triflorum* (Rose Family)
20-40 cm (8-16 in.)

This common perennial is found in dry fields and open woodlands in the prairie and mountain regions. Leaves occur in clusters at the base of the flowering stem, halfway up the stem, and just beneath the flower heads. Easily distinguished in the field by its cluster of three nodding, red-purple flowers. The flowers are succeeded in summer by a tuft of feathery plumes, for which the plant is named. Blooms April-June.

## SCARLET MALLOW
*Sphaeralcea coccinea* (Mallow Family)
to 20 cm (8 in.)

A mat-forming plant common on dry soils throughout the grassland region. Gray-green leaves have 3-5 lobes and are covered with soft hairs. Its small terminal clusters of orange, yellow-centred flowers bloom May-July.

## BALL CACTUS
*Coryphantha vivipara* (Cactus Family)
to 8 cm (3 in.)

Very common on dry soil in southern Alberta. Green, ball-shaped cactus bears numerous clusters of large prickles which serve as modified leaves. Showy pink, yellow-centred flowers bloom in July. Its flowers are succeeded by small green berries which turn brown as they mature.

## FIREWEED
*Epilobium angustifolium* (Evening Primrose Family)
1-2 m (40-80 in.)

Very common in open woodlands, clearings, and burned-out areas, it is the floral emblem of the Yukon Territory. Narrow, willow-like leaves grow along the length of the stem. Its long conical spike of bright pink, four-petalled flowers is unmistakable. Often grows in dense colonies. Blooms June-August.

## COMMON PINK WINTERGREEN
*Pyrola asarifolia* (Wintergreen Family)
20-40 cm (8-16 in.)

Found in moist woods and swampy areas throughout Alberta. Glossy, heart-shaped leaves are clustered around plant base. Its slender, red flowering stem has a long terminal cluster of up to 20 pink flowers. The delicate, bell-shaped flowers are very fragrant. Related to nine similar species. Blooms June-August.

## BOG ROSEMARY
*Andromeda polifolia* (Heath Family)
to 40 cm (16 in.)

Common in swamps and bogs in wooded areas. Shiny, slender leaves are leathery and grow along the length of the stem. Pinkish, urn-shaped flowers bloom in nodding clusters. Blooms in May-June.

## RED HEATHER
*Phyllodoce empetriformis* (Heath Family)
to 30 cm (12 in.)

This small mat-forming shrub is common at upper elevations in the mountains. Alternate, evergreen leaves are needle-like and grooved on both surfaces. Bell-shaped pink flowers bloom in nodding terminal clusters in June-July. Often grows in close association with similar species of White and Yellow Heather.

### SHOOTING STAR
*Dodecatheon pulchellum* (Primrose Family)
10-30 cm (4-12 in.)

Common on moist soil in meadows, fields, and open woodlands. Narrow leaves are widest near their tip, and grow upward from the plant base. A small cluster of beautiful red-purple flowers bloom at the tip of the red-flowering stem. The flower petals arch backward gracefully to expose the yellow stamen tube. Blooms May-July.

### COMMON RED INDIAN PAINTBRUSH
*Castilleja miniata* (Figwort Family)
to 60 cm (24 in.)

Common and widespread in woodlands and meadows in the montane and mountain regions. Alternate leaves are narrow and grow along the entire stem length. The brush-like spike atop the stem is composed of colourful bracts surrounding the inconspicuous green-yellow flowers. Alberta is home to several species of paintbrush, which range in colour from pink and orange to yellow and white. Blooms June-August.

### ELEPHANT'S HEAD
*Pedicularis groenlandica* (Figwort Family)
to 50 cm (20 in.)

Common in wet meadows and marshes in the montane and mountain regions. Dark green leaves are fern-like and finely divided. Leafy stems support long clusters of pink flowers which resemble an elephant's head and trunk. Blooms June-August.

## PINK PUSSYTOES
*Antennaria rosea* (Composite Family)
15-30 cm (6-12 in.)

Common in dry meadows and open woodlands in southern Alberta. Rounded basal leaves are covered with white hairs and have 3-5 distinct veins. The short flowering stalk bears a terminal cluster of pinkish, woolly flower heads which bloom in May-August.

## CANADA THISTLE
*Cirsium arvense* (Composite Family)
20-100 cm (8-40 in.)

A very common introduced weed found in ditches and fields throughout Alberta. Dark green leaves are scalloped and have prickly margins. Branching stem supports several small clusters of woolly, pink-mauve (occasionally white) flowers. Blooms June-August.

# BLUE AND PURPLE FLOWERS

## PRAIRIE CROCUS
*Anemone patens* (Crowfoot Family)
to 25 cm (10 in.)

Very common on dry soil in the grassland and parkland regions. Its narrowly divided leaves and fleshy stems are thickly coated with silky hairs. The conspicuous, cup-shaped purple or white flowers bloom April-June. One of our earliest spring flowers, it often appears before the snow has completely melted. It is Manitoba's floral emblem.

## TALL LARKSPUR
*Delphinium glaucum* (Crowfoot Family)
1-2 m (40-80 in.)

Common in wet woods, thickets, and along rocky slopes. Its spreading leaves have 3-5 lobes, and each lobe is cleft at its tip. Purplish to white flowers bloom in a long terminal spike. Each flower has a long spur extending backward, which is formed by the upper sepal. Poisonous. Blooms June-July.

## WILD LUPINE
*Lupinus argenteus* (Legume Family)
30-60 cm (12-24 in.)

Common on fields and roadsides in the grassland and montane regions, it typically grows in dense clusters. The leaves consist of 7-11 very narrow leaflets which radiate like wheel spokes from a central axis. Each flowering stem ends in a long terminal cluster of showy purple to lavender flowers. Blooms July-August.

## WILD VETCH
*Vicia americana* (Legume Family)
40-100 cm (16-40 in.)

Common in meadows, thickets, and open woodlands in the prairie and parkland regions. Alternate, compound leaves are divided into 8-14 oval leaflets. One-sided clusters of delicate blue-purple flowers blossom at intervals along the twining, climbing stem. Blooms June-July.

## STICKY PURPLE GERANIUM
*Geranium viscosissimum* (Geranium Family)
30-60 cm (12-24 in.)

Common in meadows, fields, and open woodlands in southern Alberta. Dark green leaves have long stalks and are divided into 5-7 coarsely toothed lobes. Both leaf stalks and flowering stem are sticky to the touch. Showy purple-pink flowers are excellent field mark. Blooms June-August.

## WILD BLUE FLAX
*Linum lewisii* (Flax Family)
20-60 cm (8-24 in.)

Found on dry hillsides and roadsides throughout southern Alberta. Alternate, narrow leaves grow along the entire stem length. Long, wiry stem terminates in small clusters of pale blue, yellow-centred flowers. Blooms June-July.

## EARLY BLUE VIOLET
*Viola adunca* (Violet Family)
5-10 cm (2-4 in.)

Very common in moist woods and meadows throughout the province. Long-stalked basal leaves are typically heart-shaped, but often variable. Leaves and flowers arise from a fleshy rootstock and have stalks which are slightly hairy. Small, five-petalled, blue-violet flowers bloom May-July. The inner edges of the petals are white and sometimes hairy.

### NORTHERN GENTIAN
*Gentianella amarella* (Gentian Family)
to 50 cm (20 in.)

Common in moist fields and thickets. Light green leaves are oblong and grow along the entire stem length. Terminal cluster of fringed, tubular flowers bloom July-September. Flowers are typically purple-blue, but may sometimes be white.

### ALPINE FORGET-ME-NOT
*Myosotis alpestris* (Borage Family)
10-30 cm (4-12 in.)

This familiar alpine flower is common in moist mountain meadows. The narrow leaves have a prominent central vein, and are stalked near the base of the plant, stalkless near the top. Distinguished at a glance by its beautiful, yellow-centred mauve flowers. Blooms June-August.

### TALL LUNGWORT
*Mertensia paniculata* (Borage Family)
30-80 cm (12-32 in.)

Common in moist meadows, thickets, and along streams. Dark green leaves are egg-shaped and hairy on both sides. Tall, supple stem supports nodding cluster of bell-shaped, bright blue flowers. Blooms May-July.

## WILD BERGAMOT
*Monarda fistulosa* var. *menthaefolia*
(Mint Family) 40-80 cm (16-32 in.)

Common in fields, meadows, and open woodlands in southern Alberta. Gray-green leaves are rounded, sharply toothed, and pointed at the tip. Conspicuous cluster of purple-pink flowers blooms in July-August. Also called Horsemint in reference to its minty odour.

## SMOOTH BLUE BEARD TONGUE
*Pentstemon nitidus* (Figwort Family)
15-50 cm (6-20 in.)

Common in dry, open areas in southern Alberta. Opposite, gray-green leaves are oval to lance-shaped and hairy on both sides. Bright blue-purple, tubular flowers bloom in loose terminal cluster in June-August. Often found growing in clumps.

## HAREBELL
*Campanula rotundifolia* (Bluebell Family)
15-50 cm (6-20 in.)

Very common on sandy or gravelly soil in a variety of habitats throughout the province. Basal leaves are rounded or heart-shaped, and often wither at the onset of flowering. Narrow stem leaves persist. Grass-like flowering stems terminate in clusters of nodding, bell-shaped flowers. Flowers are typically mauve, but blue and white variants are not uncommon. Often grows in dense clumps. Blooms June-September.

# ALBERTA SANCTUARIES

There are a host of parks, wilderness areas, and sanctuaries around the province which are helping to preserve the natural beauty of Alberta for future generations. These living museums serve as a precious heritage for the benefit, enjoyment, and education of residents and tourists alike.

For a detailed review of the natural history of different areas in the province, the book *Parks in Alberta* by Cam Finley is an excellent reference source.

## NATIONAL PARKS

There are five national parks in Alberta which are under the jurisdiction of Parks Canada.

### Banff National Park
Established in 1885, Banff became Canada's first national park when the federal government set aside an area of 26 square kilometres in order to preserve the hot springs under Sulphur Mountain. Today the park encompasses 6,640 sq. km and includes some of Canada's most famous mountain scenery.

### Jasper National Park
Jasper National Park is located in the rugged northern Rocky Mountains. Famous for its fishing and wildlife, the park has remained largely unchanged since its establishment in 1907.

### Wood Buffalo National Park
Canada's largest national park, Wood Buffalo was established in 1922 to protect a dwindling herd of rare Wood Bison. Today it is home to the largest free-roaming herd of bison in the world and is also the last known breeding grounds for the endangered Whooping Crane.

### Elk Island National Park
A wilderness oasis in the aspen-parkland region of the province, Elk Island supports herds of elk, bison, and a vast diversity of plant and bird species.

### Waterton Lakes National Park
Waterton encompasses both mountain and prairie landscapes, and has the largest lake found in the Rockies. Established in 1885, it joined with Montana's Glacier National Park in 1932 to become the world's first international peace park.

# PROVINCIAL PARKS

Alberta has 62 provincial parks which are managed by the Alberta govern-ment. Most are used for recreational activities like fishing, camping, hiking, cycling, and swimming, while others, like Dinosaur Park and Writing-On-Stone, help to preserve the province's heritage. The locations of our provincial parks are listed below. For further information on park facilities and regulations, contact Alberta Parks and Recreation or Travel Alberta.

## SOUTHERN ALBERTA (Calgary south to U.S. border)

**Beauvais Lake**
11 km west, 7 km south of
Pincher Creek

**Bow Valley**
16 km east of Canmore

**Bragg Creek**
18 km west, 20 km south of Calgary

**Chain Lakes**
40 km southwest of Nanton

**Cypress Hills**
30 km east, 35 km south of
Medicine Hat
Cypress Hills is one of the few areas
in western North America that
avoided the last glacial period
20,000 years ago. It supports some
sub-tropical species of vegetation, in
addition to a wealth of wildlife.

**Dinosaur**
8 km north, 32 km northeast of
Brooks
Proclaimed a World Heritage Site in
1979, Dinosaur Park protects one of
the most extensive dinosaur fields in
the world.

**Fish Creek**
South of Calgary city limit

**Kananaskis**
90 km west of Calgary

**Kinbrook**
13 km south, 2 km west of Brooks

**Little Bow**
20 km south, 20 km east of Vulcan

**Park Lake**
15 km north, 2 km west of
Lethbridge

**Peter Loughheed**
90 km west, 55 km south of Calgary

**Police Outpost**
16 km west, 18 km south of
Cardston

**Taber**
2 km west, 3 km north of Taber

**Tillebrook**
8 km east of Brooks

**Willow Creek**
6 km west, 8 km south of Stavely

**Woolford**
3 km northeast, 12 km southeast of
Cardston

**Writing-On-Stone**
32 km east, 10 km south of
Milk River
This park was named for the numer-ous native carvings (petroglyphs)
which decorate the cliffs along the
Milk River. Rare petroglyphs are
protected in an archaeological
preserve.

**Wyndham-Carseland**
25 km south of Strathmore

# CENTRAL ALBERTA (Edmonton south to Calgary)

**Aspen Beach**
15 km west of Lacombe

**Big Hill Springs**
8 km north, 5 km east of Cochrane

**Big Knife**
8 km west, 12 km south of
Forestburg

**Crimson Lake**
8 km west, 6 km north of
Rocky Mountain House

**Dillberry Lake**
52 km east, 20 km south of
Wainwright

**Dry Island Buffalo Jump**
12 km north, 20 km east of Trochu

**Gooseberry Lake**
2 km east, 12 km north of Consort

**Hasse Lake**
10 km west, 6 km south of
Stony Plain

**Jarvis Bay**
6 km north of Sylvan Lake

**Little Fish Lake**
18 km south, 22 km east of
Drumheller

**Ma-Me-O Beach**
40 km west of Wetaskiwin

**Midland**
2 km west of Drumheller

**Miquelon Lake**
3 km west, 26 km north of Camrose
Famous for its bird sanctuary, it is a
major gathering place for migrating
waterfowl.

**Pigeon Lake**
50 km west, 10 km north of
Wetaskiwin

**Red Lodge**
13 km south, 13 km west of Innisfail

**Rochon Sands**
10 km west, 16 km north of Stettler

**Strathcona Science**
East Edmonton city limit

**Sylvan Lake**
16 km west of Red Deer

**Vermilion**
2 km northwest of Vermilion

**Wabamun Lake**
30 km west, 2 km south of
Stony Plain

**William A. Switzer**
3 km west, 15 km north of Hinton


# NORTHERN ALBERTA (Edmonton north to N.W.T. border)

**Calling Lake**
48 km north of Athabasca

**Carson-Pegasus**
6 km west, 10 km north of
Whitecourt

**Cold Lake**
3 km east of Cold Lake

**Cross Lake**
50 km north, 20 km east of Westlock

**Garner Lake**
48 km east, 5 km north of
Smoky Lake

**Gregoire Lake**
20 km south, 10 km east of
Fort McMurray

**Hilliard's Bay**
16 km east, 20 km northeast of
High Prairie

**Lesser Slave Lake**
10 km north of Slave Lake

**Long Lake**
6 km east, 40 km northeast of Thorhild

**Moonshine Lake**
30 km west, 5 km north of Spirit River

**Moose Lake**
3 km north, 10 km west of Bonnyville

**Notikewin**
36 km north, 30 km east of Manning

**O'Brien**
10 km south of Grande Prairie

**Pembina River**
3 km east of Evansburg

**Queen Elizabeth**
3 km north, 5 km west of Grimshaw

**Saskatoon Island**
20 km west, 3 km north of Grande Prairie
One of the few nesting sites of the Trumpeter Swan. Saskatoon berries are abundant in July and August.

**Sir Winston Churchill**
10 km northeast of Lac La Biche

**Thunder Lake**
20 km west of Barrhead

**Whitney Lakes**
25 km east of Elk Point

**Williamson**
18 km west, 2 km north of Valleyview

**Winagami Lake**
16 km south, 10 km east of McClennan

**Young's Point**
25 km west, 10 km northeast of Valleyview.

# WILDERNESS AREAS

The government of Alberta established three wilderness areas in the early '60s to preserve their special beauty and to protect them from impairment in any way. Hunting, fishing, and trapping are prohibited in these areas, and no motorized vehicles or pack animals are allowed. Visitors may travel by foot only and must pack their litter out when they leave.

**White Goat Wilderness**
Located at the eastern border of Jasper and Banff national parks, this area is characterized by high mountain ranges separated by wide valleys, extensive alpine meadows and high alpine lakes.

**Siffleur Wilderness**
Bordering the northeastern edge of Banff National Park, Siffleur has several peaks exceeding an altitude of 3,000 metres which offer good mountaineering prospects.

Interesting features include large landslides, small ice-fields and hanging glaciers.

**Ghost River Wilderness**
This area bordering the eastern edge of Banff National Park is characterized by rugged mountainous terrain and large glaciated valleys. Interesting features include ice-sculpted bedrock, steep gorges, and numerous waterfalls.

# ZOOS AND WILDLIFE PARKS

### The Calgary Zoo
The second largest zoo in Canada, it is home to over 1,400 animals. Other attractions include a tropical conservatory aviary, large petting zoo, and prehistoric park featuring life-size dinosaur replicas.

### Valley Zoo - Edmonton
Features over 350 animals on a 16-acre site.

### Polar Park - 22 km SE of Sherwood Park
A reserve for cold climate animals, it features over 100 species from Canada, the USSR, and other countries.

### Alberta Wildlife Park - 12 km N of Bon Accord
Features over 100 species of animals including jaguars, tigers, giraffes and bison.

### Inglewood Bird Sanctuary - Calgary
Over 235 species of birds have been spotted on this sanctuary on the banks of the Bow River. Natural history courses are offered year-round.

### John Janzen Nature Centre - Edmonton
Features nature exhibits on flora and fauna and guided nature tours.

### Sleepy Valley Game Farm - 28 km NE of Rocky Mountain House
Features small numbers of elk, deer, mountain sheep, moose, bison, and some exotic birds and animals.

### Buffalo Paddock - Banff
This 100-acre area just north of the Banff townsite protects a herd of wood buffalo.

### Reptile World - Strathmore
60 displays feature over 250 snakes, lizards, turtles, frogs and toads.

### Sheep River Wildlife Sanctuary - 28 km W of Turner Valley
A wildlife observation blind overlooks a meadow frequently used by Bighorn Sheep and other wildlife.

# BOTANICAL CONSERVATORIES

### Muttart Conservatory - Edmonton
Four glass pyramids house a vast diversity of flora from around the world. Three of the structures feature permanent displays of flora from tropical, arid, and temperate climates, with the fourth holding special displays every few months.

### The University of Alberta Devonian Botanical Garden
25 km SW of Edmonton
Features a variety of flora including alpine and desert species, woody ornamentals, and herbs. Includes indoor showcase and Native People's Garden.

### Devonian Gardens-Calgary
This 2.5 acre indoor park features 16,000 sub-tropical and 4,000 local plants.

### Alberta Horticultural Research Centre - 4 km E of Brooks
Features extensive flower and shrub gardens and greenhouse.

### E.S. Huesis Demonstration Forest - 12 km NW of Whitecourt
This 10-sq.-km area demonstates a variety of forest management techniques. Trails wind through several forest ecosystems, wildlife habitat zones, and mechanically prepared sites.

# MUSEUMS

**Provincial Museum of Alberta - Edmonton**
Large galleries reflect Alberta's natural history with specific displays on palaeontology, zoology and geology.

**Tyrrell Museum of Palaeontology - Drumheller**
This state-of-the-art museum traces the fossil history of Alberta and features the world's most extensive display of dinosaurs. Computers, interactive displays and videos are featured throughout.

**Banff Park Museum - Banff**
Includes historic displays of birds and animals from the Western Canadian Park Region.

**The Den - Jasper**
Features over 100 specimens of native wildlife.


# CONSERVATION ASSOCIATIONS

The following organizations are recommended to readers who wish to become more involved with the conservation of our natural environment. For information on the nature societies located in your area, contact Alberta Parks and Recreation or Parks Canada.

**Canadian Nature Federation**
453 Sussex Drive, Ottawa, Ontario. K1N 6Z4

**Federation of Alberta Naturalists**
Box 1472, Edmonton, Alberta. T5J 2N5

**International Wildlife Coalition - Canada**
Box 988, Shelburne, Ontario. L0N 1S0

**Nature Conservancy of Canada**
794-A Broadview Avenue, Toronto, Ontario. M4K 2P7

**Northwest Wildlife Preservation Society**
Box 34129, Station D, Vancouver, B.C. V6J 4N3

**World Wildlife Fund**
60 St. Clair Avenue East, Toronto, Ontario. M4T 1N5

# CHECKLISTS OF COMMON ALBERTA PLANTS AND ANIMALS

**KINGDOM PLANTAE**
DIVISION SPERMATOPHYTA
SUBDIVISION GYMNOSPERMAE
CLASS CONIFERAE - CONIFERS
FAMILY PINACEAE
____ Whitebark Pine
____ Limber Pine
____ Western White Pine
____ Jack Pine
____ Lodgepole Pine
____ Alpine Larch
____ Tamarack
____ Black Spruce
____ White Spruce
____ Engelmann Spruce
____ Balsam Fir
____ Subalpine Fir
FAMILY CUPRESSACEAE
____ Ground Juniper
____ Rocky Mountain Juniper
____ Creeping Juniper
SUBDIVISION ANGIOSPERMAE
CLASS MONOCOTYLEDONEAE
FAMILY TYPHACEAE - CATTAIL
____ Common Cattail
FAMILY LILIACEAE - LILIES
____ Nodding Onion
____ Fairy Bells
____ Glacier Lily
____ Western Wood Lily
____ Star-flowered Solomon's Seal
____ False Asphodel
____ White Camas
FAMILY ORCHIDACEAE - ORCHIDS
____ Venus' Slipper
____ Yellow Lady's Slipper
____ Northern Green Bog Orchid
____ Round-leaved Orchid
CLASS DICOTYLEDONEAE
FAMILY SALICACEAE - WILLOWS & ALLIES
____ Balsam Poplar
____ Narrowleaf Cottonwood
____ Trembling Aspen
____ Bebb's Willow

_____ Sandbar Willow
_____ Pussy Willow
_____ Scouler Willow
_____ Weeping Willow

FAMILY BETULACEAE - BIRCHES & ALLIES
_____ Green Alder
_____ Mountain Alder
_____ Water Birch
_____ Paper Birch
_____ Beaked Hazelnut

FAMILY URTICACEAE - NETTLES
_____ Common Nettle

FAMILY CHENOPODIACEAE - GOOSEFOOTS & ALLIES
_____ Lamb's Quarters
_____ Russian Thistle

FAMILY CARYOPHYLLACEAE - PINK FAMILY
_____ Field Chickweed

FAMILY NYMPHAEACEAE - WATER LILIES
_____ Yellow Pond Lily

FAMILY RANUNCULACEAE - CROWFOOTS & ALLIES
_____ Red and White Baneberry
_____ Canada Anemone
_____ Marsh Marigold
_____ Creeping Buttercup
_____ Tall Buttercup
_____ Veiny Meadow Rue
_____ Prairie Crocus
_____ Tall Larkspur

FAMILY CRUCIFERAE - MUSTARDS & ALLIES
_____ Penny Cress
_____ Wild Mustard

FAMILY PARNASSIACEAE - GRASS-OF-PARNASSUS
_____ Grass of Parnassus

FAMILY GROSSULARIACEAE - GOOSEBERRIES, CURRANTS & ALLIES
_____ Northern Gooseberry
_____ Wild Black Currant

FAMILY ROSACEAE - ROSE FAMILY
_____ Yellow Dryad
_____ Shrubby Cinquefoil
_____ Prickly Wild Rose
_____ Common Wild Rose
_____ Old Man's Whiskers
_____ Pin Cherry
_____ Red Choke Cherry
_____ Wild Red Raspberry
_____ European Mountain Ash
_____ Saskatoon Serviceberry

FAMILY LEGUMINOSAE - PEAS & ALLIES
_____ White Clover
_____ White Pea Vine
_____ Early Yellow Locoweed
_____ Wild Lupine

_____ Wild Vetch

**FAMILY GERANIACEAE - GERANIUMS**
_____ Wild White Geranium
_____ Sticky Purple Geranium

**FAMILY LINACEAE - FLAX**
_____ Wild Blue Flax

**FAMILY ACERACEAE - MAPLES**
_____ Douglas Maple

**FAMILY MALVACEAE - MALLOWS**
_____ Scarlet Mallow

**FAMILY VIOLACEAE - VIOLETS**
_____ Western Canada Violet
_____ Early Blue Violet

**FAMILY CACTACEAE - CACTUS**
_____ Prickly Pear Cactus
_____ Ball Cactus

**FAMILY ELAEAGNACEAE - OLEASTER FAMILY**
_____ Silverberry
_____ Canadian Buffalo-berry

**FAMILY ONAGRACEAE - EVENING PRIMROSE FAMILY**
_____ Yellow Evening Primrose
_____ Fireweed

**FAMILY UMBELLIFERAE - CARROT FAMILY**
_____ Cow Parsnip

**FAMILY CORNACEAE - DOGWOODS**
_____ Bunchberry
_____ Red Osier Dogwood

**FAMILY PYROLACEAE - WINTERGREENS**
_____ Common Pink Wintergreen

**FAMILY ERICACEAE - HEATH**
_____ Labrador Tea
_____ Bog Rosemary
_____ Red Heather
_____ Dwarf Blueberry

**FAMILY PRIMULACEAE - PRIMROSES**
_____ Fairy Candelabra
_____ Shooting Star

**FAMILY GENTIANACEAE - GENTIANS**
_____ Northern Gentian

**FAMILY MENYANTHACEAE - BUCK-BEAN**
_____ Buck-bean

**FAMILY CONVOLVULACEAE - MORNING-GLORY**
_____ Wild Morning-glory

**FAMILY POLEMONIACEAE - PHLOX FAMILY**
_____ Moss Phlox

**FAMILY BORAGINACEAE - BORAGE FAMILY**
_____ Yellow Puccoon
_____ Alpine Forget-me-not
_____ Tall Lungwort

**FAMILY LABIATAE - MINTS**
_____ Wild Bergamot

**FAMILY SCROPHULARIACEAE - FIGWORT FAMILY**

_____ Yellow Toad-flax
_____ Western Lousewort
_____ Common Red Indian Paint-brush
_____ Elephant's Head
_____ Smooth Blue Beard-tongue

FAMILY LENTIBULARIACEAE - BLADDERWORTS
_____ Common Bladderwort

FAMILY PLANTAGINACEAE - PLANTAINS
_____ Common Plantain

FAMILY RUBIACEAE - MADDER FAMILY
_____ Northern Bedstraw

FAMILY CAPRIFOLIACEAE - HONEYSUCKLE FAMILY
_____ Low-bush Cranberry
_____ Twining Honeysuckle
_____ Bracted Honeysuckle
_____ Buckbrush
_____ Snowberry

FAMILY CAMPANULACEAE - BLUEBELLS
_____ Harebell

FAMILY COMPOSITAE - COMPOSITE FAMILY
_____ Arrow-leaved Coltsfoot
_____ Common Yarrow
_____ Heart-leaved Arnica
_____ Wild Gaillardia
_____ Common Dandelion
_____ False Dandelion
_____ Prairie Coneflower
_____ Tall Smooth Goldenrod
_____ Annual Sunflower
_____ Pink Pussytoes
_____ Canada Thistle

# KINGDOM ANIMALIA
## SECTION DEUTEROSTOMIA
## PHYLUM CHORDATA
## SUBPHYLUM VERTEBRATA
### CLASS OSTEICHTHYES - BONY FISHES
### ORDER OSTEOGLOSSIFORMES
FAMILY HIODONTIDAE - MOONEYE
_____ Goldeye

### ORDER SALMONIFORMES - SALMON, TROUT & PIKES
FAMILY SALMONIDAE - SALMON & ALLIES
_____ Brown Trout
_____ Rainbow Trout
_____ Cutthroat Trout
_____ Lake Trout
_____ Brook Trout
_____ Bull Trout

_____ Cisco

_____ Lake Whitefish

_____ Mountain Whitefish

_____ Arctic Grayling

FAMILY ESOCIDAE - PIKE

_____ Northern Pike

## ORDER CYPRINIFORMES - MINNOW-LIKE FISHES
FAMILY CATOSTOMIDAE - SUCKERS

_____ White Sucker

_____ Longnose Sucker

FAMILY CYPRINIDAE - MINNOWS & ALLIES

_____ Lake Chub

_____ Fathead Minnow

_____ Spottail Shiner

## ORDER PERCOPSIFORMES
FAMILY PERCOPSIDAE - TROUT-PERCHES

_____ Trout-Perch

## ORDER GADIFORMES - COD-LIKE FISHES
FAMILY GADIDAE - COD

_____ Burbot

## ORDER GASTEROSTEIFORMES
FAMILY GASTEROSTEIDAE - STICKLEBACKS

_____ Brook Stickleback

## ORDER PERCIFORMES - PERCH-LIKE FISHES
FAMILY PERCIDAE - PERCHES

_____ Yellow Perch

_____ Sauger

_____ Walleye

# CLASS AMPHIBIA - AMPHIBIANS
## ORDER CAUDATA - SALAMANDERS
FAMILY AMBYSTOMIDAE - MOLE SALAMANDERS

_____ Tiger Salamander

## ORDER SALIENTIA - FROGS AND TOADS
FAMILY BUFONIDAE - TRUE TOADS

_____ Canadian Toad

_____ Boreal Toad

FAMILY HYLIDAE - TREE AND GRASS FROGS

_____ Boreal Chorus Frog

FAMILY RANIDAE - TRUE FROGS

_____ Wood Frog

# CLASS REPTILIA - REPTILES
## ORDER TESTUDINES - TURTLES
FAMILY EMYDIDAE - FRESHWATER & BOX TURTLES

_____ Painted Turtle

## ORDER SQUAMATA - SNAKES & LIZARDS
SUBORDER LACERTILIA - LIZARDS

FAMILY IGUANIDAE - IGUANAS

_____ Short-horned Lizard

SUBORDER SERPENTES - SNAKES

FAMILY COLUBRIDAE - HARMLESS SNAKES

_____ Red-sided Garter Snake

_____ Plains Garter Snake
_____ Wandering Garter Snake
_____ Bullsnake
FAMILY VIPERIDAE - PIT VIPERS
_____ Prairie Rattlesnake

# CLASS AVES
## ORDER GAVIIFORMES
FAMILY GAVIIDAE - LOONS
_____ Common Loon

## ORDER PODICIPEDIFORMES
FAMILY PODICIPEDIDAE - GREBES
_____ Horned Grebe
_____ Eared Grebe
_____ Red-necked Grebe
_____ Pied-billed Grebe

## ORDER CICONIIFORMES
FAMILY ARDEIDAE - HERONS AND BITTERNS
_____ Great Blue Heron
_____ American Bittern

## ORDER ANSERIFORMES - WATERFOWL
FAMILY ANATIDAE - GEESE, DUCKS & ALLIES
SUBFAMILY ANSERINAE - GEESE
_____ Canada Goose
_____ Snow Goose
SUBFAMILY ANATINAE - SURFACE-FEEDING DUCKS
_____ Mallard
_____ Blue-winged Teal
_____ Green-winged Teal
_____ American Widgeon
_____ Northern Shoveler
_____ Gadwall
_____ Pintail
_____ Redhead
_____ Ring-necked Duck
_____ Canvasback
_____ Lesser Scaup
_____ Common Goldeneye
_____ Bufflehead
_____ Harlequin Duck
_____ White-winged Scoter
_____ Common Merganser
_____ Ruddy Duck

## ORDER FALCONIFORMES - VULTURES, HAWKS & FALCONS
FAMILY ACCIPITRIDAE - KITES, HAWKS & EAGLES
_____ Red-tailed Hawk
_____ Swainson's Hawk
_____ Northern Harrier
FAMILY FALCONIDAE - FALCONS
_____ American Kestrel
_____ Merlin

## ORDER GALLIFORMES - CHICKEN-LIKE BIRDS

FAMILY PHASIANIDAE - QUAIL, PARTRIDGES, PHEASANTS & GROUSE
____ Ruffed Grouse
____ Sharp-tailed Grouse
____ Ring-necked Pheasant
____ Gray Partridge

## ORDER GRUIFORMES
FAMILY RALLIDAE - COOTS & RAILS
____ American Coot

## ORDER CHARADRIIFORMES - SHOREBIRDS, GULLS & ALLIES
FAMILY CHARADRIIDAE - PLOVERS
____ Killdeer
FAMILY RECURVIROSTRIDAE - AVOCETS
____ American Avocet
FAMILY SCOLOPACIDAE - SANDPIPERS & PHALAROPES
SUBFAMILY SCOLOPACINAE - SANDPIPERS
____ Common Snipe
____ Spotted Sandpiper
____ Greater Yellowlegs
____ Willet
____ Marbled Godwit
____ Long-billed Curlew
____ Lesser Yellowlegs
____ Least Sandpiper
____ Long-billed Dowitcher
SUBFAMILY PHALAROPODINAE PHALAROPES
____ Wilson's Phalarope
FAMILY LARIDAE - GULLS AND TERNS
SUBFAMILY LARINAE
____ Franklin's Gull
____ Ring-billed Gull
____ California Gull
____ Herring Gull
SUBFAMILY STERNINAE
____ Black Tern
____ Common Tern

## ORDER COLUMBIFORMES
FAMILY COLUMBIDAE - PIGEONS & DOVES
____ Rock Dove
____ Mourning Dove

## ORDER STRIGIFORMES
FAMILY STRIGIDAE - OWLS
____ Burrowing Owl
____ Short-eared Owl
____ Great Horned Owl

## ORDER APODIFORMES
FAMILY TROCHILIDAE - HUMMINGBIRDS
____ Ruby-throated Hummingbird
____ Rufous Hummingbird

## ORDER CORACIIFORMES
FAMILY ALCEDINIDAE - KINGFISHERS
____ Belted Kingfisher

## ORDER PICIFORMES
### FAMILY PICIDAE - WOODPECKERS
___ Northern Flicker
___ Downy Woodpecker
___ Hairy Woodpecker
___ Yellow-bellied Sapsucker

## ORDER PASSERIFORMES - PERCHING BIRDS
### FAMILY TYRANNIDAE -FLYCATCHERS
___ Eastern Kingbird
___ Eastern Phoebe
___ Western Wood Peewee
___ Least Flycatcher
### FAMILY ALAUDIDAE - LARKS
___ Horned Lark
### FAMILY HIRUNDINIDAE - SWALLOWS
___ Bank Swallow
___ Tree Swallow
___ Barn Swallow
___ Cliff Swallow
___ Purple Martin
### FAMILY CORVIDAE - CROWS & ALLIES
___ Gray Jay
___ Blue Jay
___ Common Crow
___ Common Raven
___ Black-billed Magpie
### FAMILY PARIDAE - CHICKADEES
___ Black-capped Chickadee
___ Boreal Chickadee
### FAMILY SITTIDAE - NUTHATCHES
___ Red-breasted Nuthatch
### FAMILY TROGLODYTIDAE - WRENS
___ House Wren
### FAMILY MUSCICAPIDAE - KINGLETS, THRUSHES & ALLIES
#### SUBFAMILY SYLVIINAE - KINGLETS
___ Ruby-crowned Kinglet
#### SUBFAMILY TURDINAE - THRUSHES & BLUEBIRDS
___ American Robin
___ Swainson's Thrush
___ Mountain Bluebird
### FAMILY BOMBYCILLIDAE - WAXWINGS
___ Cedar Waxwing
___ Bohemian Waxwing
### FAMILY LANIIDAE - SHRIKES
___ Loggerhead Shrike
### FAMILY STURNIDAE - STARLINGS
___ Common Starling
### FAMILY VIREONIDAE - VIREOS
___ Red-eyed Vireo
### FAMILY EMBERIZIDAE - WOOD WARBLERS, SPARROWS, BLACKBIRDS, MEADOWLARKS & ORIOLES

SUBFAMILY PARULINAE - WOOD WARBLERS
____ Yellow Warbler
____ Tennessee Warbler
____ Blackpoll Warbler
____ Yellow-rumped Warbler
____ American Redstart
____ Ovenbird

SUBFAMILY EMBERIZINAE - SPARROWS
____ Savannah Sparrow
____ Vesper Sparrow
____ Dark-eyed Junco
____ Clay-colored Sparrow
____ Chipping Sparrow
____ White-throated Sparrow
____ Song Sparrow

SUBFAMILY ICTERINAE - BLACKBIRDS & ALLIES
____ Western Meadowlark
____ Northern Oriole
____ Red-winged Blackbird
____ Brewer's Blackbird
____ Common Grackle
____ Brown-headed Cowbird

FAMILY FRINGILLIDAE - FINCHES
____ Common Redpoll
____ Pine Siskin
____ American Goldfinch
____ Red Crossbill

FAMILY PASSERIDAE - WEAVER FINCHES
____ House Sparrow

## CLASS MAMMALIA - MAMMALS
## ORDER INSECTIVORA - INSECTIVORES
FAMILY SORICIDAE - SHREWS
____ Masked Shrew

## ORDER CHIROPTERA - BATS
FAMILY VESPERTILIONIDAE - PLAIN-NOSE BATS
____ Little Brown Bat
____ Big Brown Bat

## ORDER LAGOMORPHA - RABBIT-LIKE MAMMALS
FAMILY OCHOTONIDAE - PIKAS
____ Rocky Mountain Pika

FAMILY LEPORIDAE - HARES AND RABBITS
____ Nuttall's Cottontail
____ Snowshoe Hare
____ White-tailed Prairie Hare

## ORDER RODENTIA - RODENTS
FAMILY SCIURIDAE - SQUIRRELS
____ Least Chipmunk
____ Yellow Pine Chipmunk
____ Woodchuck
____ Hoary Marmot
____ Richardson's Ground Squirrel

___ Columbian Ground Squirrel
___ Golden-mantled Ground Squirrel
___ Thirteen-lined Ground Squirrel
___ Eastern Gray Squirrel
___ Red Squirrel
___ Northern Flying Squirrel

FAMILY GEOMYIDAE - POCKET GOPHERS
___ Northern Pocket Gopher

FAMILY CASTORIDAE - BEAVER
___ Beaver

FAMILY MURIDAE - MICE, RATS & VOLES
___ Deer Mouse
___ Bushy-tailed Woodrat
___ Southern Boreal Red-backed Vole
___ Muskrat
___ House Mouse

FAMILY ZAPODIDAE - JUMPING MICE
___ Western Jumping Mouse

FAMILY ERETHIZONTIDAE - PORCUPINE
___ Porcupine

## ORDER CARNIVORA - CARNIVORES

FAMILY CANIDAE - DOGS
___ Coyote
___ Gray Wolf
___ Red Fox

FAMILY URSIDAE- BEARS
___ Black Bear
___ Grizzly Bear

FAMILY PROCYONIDAE - RACCOONS & ALLIES
___ Raccoon

FAMILY MUSTELIDAE - WEASELS & ALLIES
___ Ermine
___ Long-tailed Weasel
___ Mink
___ Badger
___ Striped Skunk

FAMILY FELIDAE- CATS
___ Mountain Lion
___ Canada Lynx

## ORDER ARTIODACTYLA - CLOVEN-HOOFED MAMMALS

FAMILY CERVIDAE - DEER
___ Elk
___ Mule Deer
___ White-tailed Deer
___ Moose

FAMILY ANTILOCAPRIDAE - PRONGHORN
___ Pronghorn

FAMILY BOVIDAE - BISON & ALLIES
___ Bison
___ Mountain Goat
___ Bighorn Sheep

# GLOSSARY

**Alternate:** spaced singly along the stem.

**Anther:** the part of the stamen that produces pollen.

**Albino:** an animal lacking external pigmentation.

**Annual:** a plant which completes its life cycle in one year.

**Anterior:** pertaining to the front end.

**Aquatic:** living in water.

**Ascending:** rising or curving upward.

**Barbel:** an organ near the mouth of fish used as an organ of taste, touch, or smell.

**Berry:** a fruit formed from a single ovary which is fleshy or pulpy and contains one or many seeds.

**Bloom:** a whitish, powdery or waxy covering.

**Bract:** a scale or leaf, usually small.

**Branchlet:** a twig from which leaves grow.

**Boss:** a rounded knob between the eyes of some toads.

**Burrow:** a tunnel excavated and inhabited by an animal.

**Carnivorous:** feeding primarily on meat.

**Catkin:** a spike of small flowers.

**Cold-blooded:** refers to animals which are unable to regulate their own body temperature. This designation is considered inappropriate by many since cold-blooded species are capable of maintaining temperatures as high, or higher, than endotherms (see below) on warm days.

**Compound Leaf:** a leaf divided into two or more leaf-like parts (leaflets).

**Deciduous:** shedding annually.

**Diurnal:** active primarily during the day.

**Dorsal:** pertaining to the back or upper surface.

**Ecology:** the study of the relationships between organisms, and between organisms and their environment.

**Ectotherm:** an animal which regulates its body temperature behaviourly from outside sources of heat, e.g., the sun.

**Endotherm:** an animal which regulates its body temperature internally (formerly referred to as a warm-blooded animal).

**Flower stalk:** the stem bearing the flowers.

**Fruit**: the matured, seed-bearing ovary.

**Habitat**: the physical area in which organisms live.

**Herbivorous**: feeding primarily on vegetation.

**Insectivorous**: feeding primarily on insects.

**Invertebrate**: animals lacking backbones, e.g., worms, slugs, crayfish, shrimps.

**Lance-shaped**: a leaf which is much longer than it is broad, widest near its base, and tapered at the tip.

**Larva**: immature forms of an animal which differ from the adult.

**Lateral**: located away from the mid line, at or near the sides.

**Lobe**: a projecting part of a leaf or flower, usually rounded.

**Nest**: A structure built for shelter or insulation.

**Nocturnal**: active primarily at night.

**Omnivorous**: feeding on both animal and vegetable food.

**Ovary**: the female sex organ which is the site of egg production and maturation.

**Perennial**: a plant that lives for several years.

**Petal**: the coloured outer parts of a flower head.

**Piscivorous**: feeding primarily on fish.

**Pistil**: the central organ of the flower which develops into a fruit.

**Pollen**: The tiny grains produced in the anthers which contain the male reproductive cells.

**Posterior**: pertaining to the rear.

**Sepal**: the outer, usually green, leaf-like structures that protect the flower bud and are located at the base of an open flower.

**Species**: a group of interbreeding organisms which are reproductively isolated from other groups.

**Spur**: a pointed projection.

**Subspecies**: a relatively uniform, distinct portion of a species population.

**Suckering**: method of tree and shrub reproduction when shoots arise from an underground stem.

**Ungulate**: an animal that has hooves.

**Ventral**: of or on the abdomen (belly).

**Vertebrate**: an animal possessing a backbone.

**Warm-blooded**: an animal which regulates its blood temperature internally. Endotherm is the preferred designation for this characteristic.

**Whorl**: a circle of leaves or flowers about a stem.

**Woolly**: bearing long or matted hairs.

# REFERENCES

## FLORA

Budd, A.C. *Budd's Flora of the Canadian Prairie Provinces.* Agriculture Canada, Hull, Que., 1987.

Brockman, C.F. *Trees of North America.* Golden Press, N.Y., 1979.

Claid, L.J. *Wildflowers of the Pacific Northwest.* Gray's Publishing, Sidney, B.C., 1976.

Cormack, R. *Wildflowers of Alberta.* Hurtig Publishers, Edmonton, 1977.

Crittenden, M. *Trees of the West.* Celestial Arts, Millburne, Calif., 1977.

Elias, T.S. *Trees of North America.* Van Nostrand Reinhold Co., N.Y., 1980.

Hosie, R.C. *Native Trees of Canada.* Fitzhenry and Whiteside, Don Mills, 1979.

Inkpen, W., and Van Eyk, R. *Guide to Common Native Trees and Shrubs in Alberta.* Alberta Environment, Edmonton, 1988.

Lyons, C.P. *Trees, Shrubs and Flowers to Know in British Columbia.* Evergreen Press Ltd., Vancouver, 1965.

Mohlenbrock, R.H., Thieret, J.W. *Trees.* MacMillan Pub. Co., N.Y. 1987.

Moss, E.H., and Packer, J.G. *Flora of Alberta.* University of Toronto Press, Toronto, 1983.

Pesman, M.W. *Meet the Natives. A Beginner's Field Guide to Rocky Mountain Wild Flowers, Trees and Shrubs.* Pruett Publishers, Denver, 1988.

Porsild, A.E. *Rocky Mountain Wildflowers.* National Museums of Canada, Ottawa, 1984.

Preston, R. *Rocky Mountain Trees.* Dover Publications Inc., N.Y., 1968.

Scagel, R.F.; Bandoni, R.J.; Rouse, G.F.; Schofield, W.B.; Stein, J.R.; and Maze J.R. *Plants. An Evolutionary Survey.* Wadsworth Pub. Co., Belmont, California, 1984.

Scotter, G.W. and Flygare, H. *Wildflowers of the Canadian Rockies.* Hurtig Publishers, Edmonton, 1986.

Spellenberg, R. *The Audubon Society Field Guide to North American Wildflowers.* A. Knopf, N.Y., 1979.

Vance, F.R.; Jowsey, J.R., and McClean, J.S. *Wildflowers Across the Prairies.* Western Producer Prairie Books, Saskatoon, Sask., 1986.

Venning, D. *Wildflowers of North America.* Golden Press, N.Y., 1984.

## BIRDS

Godfrey, W.E. *The Birds of Canada.* Queen's Printer, Ottawa, 1986.

May, C.P. *A Book of Canadian Birds.* MacMillan of Canada, Toronto, 1967.

Miklos, D.F. *The Audubon Society Field Guide to North American Birds.* A. Knopf, N.Y., 1977.

Peterson, R.T. *A Field Guide to the Western Birds.* Houghton Mifflin Co., Boston, 1961.

Robbins, C.S.; Bruun,B., and Zim, H.S. *Birds of North America.* Golden Press, N.Y., 1984.

Salt, W.R. and Salt, J.R. *The Birds of Alberta.* Hurtig Publishers, Edmonton, 1976.

Savage, C. *The Wonder of Canadian Birds.* Western Producer Prairie Books, Saskatoon, 1985.

Taverner, P.A. *Birds of Canada.* National Museums of Canada, Ottawa, 1934.

# MAMMALS

Banfield, A.W. *The Mammals of Canada*. University of Toronto Press, Toronto, 1987.

Burt, W.H., and Grossenheider, R.P. *A Field Guide to the Mammals of America North of Mexico*. Houghton Mifflin, Boston, 1976.

Walker, E.P. *Mammals of the World*. Johns Hopkins University Press, Baltimore, 1975.

Whitaker, J.D. *The Audubon Society Field Guide to North American Mammals*. A. Knopf, N.Y., 1980.

Wooding, F.H. *Wild Mammals of Canada*. McGraw Hill Ryerson, Toronto, 1982.

Wrigley, R.E. *Mammals in North America*. Hyperion Press, Winnipeg, 1986.

# REPTILES AND AMPHIBIANS

Behler, J.L. and King, F.W. *The Audubon Society Field Guide to North American Reptiles and Amphibians*. A. Knopf, N.Y., 1979.

Cook, F. *Introduction to Canadian Amphibians and Reptiles*. National Museums of Canada, Ottawa, 1984.

Froom, B. *Snakes of Canada*. McClelland and Stewart, Toronto, 1972.

Stebbins, R.C. *Amphibians and Reptiles of Western North America*. Houghton Mifflin Co., Boston, 1985.

Zim, H.S. and Smith, H.M. *Reptiles and Amphibians. A Guide to Familiar American Species*. Golden Press, N.Y., 1956.

# FISH

McAllister, D.E. and Crossman, E.J. *A Guide to the Freshwater Sport Fishes of Canada*. National Museums of Canada, Ottawa, 1973.

Paetz, M. and Nelson, J. *The Fishes of Alberta*. Queen's Printer, Edmonton, 1970.

Thompson, Peter. *Thompson's Guide to Freshwater Fishes*. Houghton Mifflin Co., Boston, 1985.

Zim, H.S. *Fishes. A Guide to Familiar American Species*. Simon and Schuster, N.Y., 1956.

# ECOLOGY

Ford, J.M., and Monroe, J.M. *Living Systems, Principles and Relationships*. Canfield Press, San Francisco, 1977.

Franke, R.G. *Man and the Changing Environment*. Holt, Rinehart and Winston, Toronto, 1975.

Hardy, W.G. *Alberta. A Natural History*. Evergreen Press, Vancouver, 1967.

Keeton, W.T. *Biological Science*. Norton and Company, N.Y., 1980.

Lawrence, R.D. *The Natural History of Canada*. Key Porter, Toronto, 1988.

Spalding, D.A.E. *A Nature Guide to Alberta*. Hurtig Publishers, Edmonton, 1980.

# INDEX

# ABOUT THE AUTHOR

A former resident of Calgary, Edmonton and Didsbury, James Kavanagh is a writer, naturalist and Notre Dame fan. After working as an advertising copywriter for several years, he decided to work as a free-lance writer instead and focus his energies on promoting conservation instead of consumption. A member of numerous conservation societies, he has a B.Sc. in Zoology from the University of Alberta. This book is a result of his desire to create a field guide that is accessible to everyone who wants to know more about their world.

The following titles are also published by Lone Pine Publishing:

## BIRDS OF EDMONTON
## BIRDS OF CALGARY

Two guides to identify common and rare birds found in and around the cities of Edmonton and Calgary. Fascinating details about the habits and habitats of urban birds and their methods of adaptation are included.

**ISBN 0-919433-80-4 Edmonton**
**ISBN 0-919433-82-0 Calgary**

5 1/2 x 8 1/2   softcover   **$9.95**


## ANIMAL TRACKS OF WESTERN CANADA

This easy-to-use guide to the tracks of Western Canada's most common animals makes identification a detective game. Includes the tracks of nearly sixty animals including squirrels, deer and wolves.

**ISBN 0-919433-20-0**

4 1/4 x 5 3/4   softcover   **$6.95**


## ALBERTA WILDLIFE VIEWING GUIDE

Take a walk on the wild side using this comprehensive guide to more than sixty of Alberta's finest wildlife viewing sites. Includes information on where to look for Alberta's special species, seasonal indicators, tips on wildlife photography, maps and photos.

**ISBN 0-919433-78-2**

5 1/2 x 8 1/2   softcover   **$7.95**


## DISCOVERER'S GUIDE TO ELK ISLAND

Designed to help you identify the common plants, birds, mammals and habitats of Elk Island National Park, this guide book also includes information on trails and history of the area.

**ISBN 0-919433-89-8**

5 1/2 x 8 1/2   softcover   **$8.95**


Look for these books at your local bookstore. If unavailable, order direct from Lone Pine Publishing, 206, 10426-81 Ave, Edmonton, Alberta  T6E 1X5
Phone: (403) 433-9333  Fax: (403) 433 9646